Baby Alarm!

Baby Alarm!

A Neurotic's Guide to Fatherhood

John Crace

VISTA

First Published in Great Britain 1996
as a Vista paperback original

Vista is an imprint of the Cassell Group
Wellington House, 125 Strand, London WC2R 0BB

A catalogue record for this book is available from the British Library

ISBN 0 575 60054 3

Designed and typeset
by Fishtail Design

Printed and bound in Great Britain by
Cox & Wyman Ltd, Reading, Berkshire

96 97 98 99   10 9 8 7 6 5 4 3 2 1

For my family

WHY?

Dear Marje
Why oh why oh why oh why do I want to be a dad?

Dear John
Buggered if I know.

Not much help there, then.

It had started as a sort of noise in the back of my head, which I mistook at first for either tinnitus or a brain tumour. Several trips to the doctor and a CAT scan later, I realized it wasn't so much a noise as a disembodied voice; and the voice was saying 'children'. If anything this was even more disturbing than a brain tumour. At least some tumours go away. Which is more than could be said for the voice.

All of which was something of a surprise, as up till then I'd gone through my whole life hardly giving children a second thought. There had been the odd panic when a girlfriend had been late with her period, but denial has always been one of my strong points, and when the scare was over I always managed to get back to forgetting that sex had anything to do with making babies. It's not that I never thought I would be a dad, it's just that I never imagined I would have to think about it.

In my dad's day, becoming a father was something that simply happened to you. You went to school, fought a war – who is it this time? Oh, it's the Germans again – came home, got a job, got married, had children. End of story. You never even had much say in how many children, because that sort of thing got left to the wife. As the youngest of three, this last point has always left me feeling particularly anxious. What if my mum decided to have me just so as to irritate my dad? It's bad enough being thought of as something of a joke later on in life, without having been born one.

The idea of children entered my consciousness at about the time when I'd got round to doing all those things that people are supposed to have done several years earlier. Most of my twenties had passed in a bit of a blur in front of the TV and it wasn't until my early thirties that I finally collected the full set of stable relationship, home, and something approximating a career. An initial feeling of relief that I had finally caught up with my friends, and that I would no longer have to lie about what I was up to, had quickly given way to something far more worrying. So I had a job, a home and a wife. Big deal. I felt pretty useless; besides which, I was still going to die.

Thoughts of my own mortality had begun increasingly to preoccupy me. When I was twenty death had been

something I'd been able to ignore. Of course, I knew I would die one day, but it seemed so far away that I felt as if I was going to live for ever. Now my body was giving me definite signs that there was no escape. My hitherto pristine brown rug was growing grey at the temples, and while I could try to kid myself that I was just losing a yard or two of pace on the football field, the scales were telling me that I was getting fat. I had to face it – no one was ever going to take a bung to get me to partner Cantona up front. This may seem like a dreary mid-life crisis to you, but to me it was very frightening.

Children offered the perfect way out. Not only would I get my very own baby to love and to hold, and who, at least initially, would think I was the funniest, cleverest, handsomest man alive, but it also offered the chance of immortality. Children were  the biological equivalent of vanity publishing. My children would have my genes; in some ways they would look like me, think like me and if they too went on to have children then part of me could go on living for years to come. Reincarnation opened up exciting possibilities. Anything I didn't particularly like about my life I had the opportunity to change with my children. So my parents had botched my education, and hadn't bought me enough Action Man paraphernalia. No problem. It could all be sorted out with my children. They could go to the right schools and get the firefighter's outfit I'd always craved. They might go on to have lives and personalities of their own but, tucked away somewhere inside them, would be a new improved me.

Self-perpetuation isn't the most noble of ambitions, and I looked hard for other, more compelling reasons for becoming a father. But I couldn't find any. I knew that the world was hideously over-populated, that some genocidal maniac could nuke the place at any time, and that even if my children somehow made it through to adulthood there would be precious few jobs for them unless I changed my surname to Windsor or possibly Coren. Any sane person would have abandoned thoughts of fatherhood there and then, but I was going to plough on regardless. My children might come to depend on me once they were born, but right now my need for them was far greater than theirs for me.

Babies aren't the sort of thing you can embark on single-handed, so I proceeded to enlist my wife's co-operation.

'Let's have a baby.'

'Why?'

Wait a minute. This wasn't right. The conversation was meant to have gone along the lines of, 'Let's have a baby.' 'Good idea.' The End. Now here she was wanting a metaphysical debate.

'Because I'm oversleeping and I'm earning too much.' I can be annoying, too.

'Very funny. I'm serious. Why do you want a baby?'

The truth wasn't likely to impress my wife overly, so I extemporized.

'I don't know really. I just feel that I've got something to give a child right now.'

This was, apparently, a satisfactory answer because my wife's face softened noticeably, but even so it wasn't quite good enough to do the trick. Like me, she had always rather assumed that we would have children one day, but she had a good job that she enjoyed and could see no earthly reason why that day should have arrived now.

'I want one too, but I think we should wait a bit.'

Action was needed. Puking infants and wild-eyed, greasy-haired parents aren't the best advertisement for the joys of motherhood, so I decided to keep my wife away from our friends with babies, and set out to ignite her dormant maternal feelings with my own brand of pessimism. She, too, had to realize that she was going to die some time. When she got a cough, I said 'lung cancer'; when she woke up with a stiff neck, I diagnosed Parkinson's. Hypochondria is a highly contagious disease and within a year I had persuaded her that she was never going to be further from death than she was then, and thereby got her agreement to start a family.

Children, then, were to be my Faustian pact. In exchange for both the promise of immortality and freedom from my existential angst, I was ready – well, sort of – to take on all the financial and material privations of fatherhood. What I hadn't bargained for was the psychological cost.

FRAIDS

'This is the National Aids Helpline. Can I help you?'

'Er . . . my partner and I want to start a family and, well, I had a number of relationships and a few flings before we met and, um, I never really bothered about safe sex because nobody did then and, er, I was wondering if I was at any risk.'

What I want the charming Scottish voice on the other end of the phone to say is that everything is going to be all right. Instead I get some measured, responsible advice.

'Heterosexual sex is not a high-risk activity, but there are dangers of HIV infection.'

Damn.

I suppose that when couples meet up nowadays they practise safe sex for a few months and then go along to the clinic together and get tested. But it wasn't quite like that when my wife and I met up. You kind of got together, went to bed a few times, and if you still liked each other then you decided you were having a relationship. The sex didn't have to be planned with military precision because Aids was still seen very much as something that happened to gays and junkies.

Over the years I did start to get the odd psychic niggle. As more became known about hetty HIV, the more decidedly iffy some of my affairs began to seem. Memories that had hitherto served as glorious sexual fantasies to while away a lonely five minutes now took on a more nightmarish quality. By now, though, my wife and I had started to practise safe sex – not as a protection against Aids, but as a form of contraception because the pill and the IUD were health risks and I didn't have the self-control for withdrawal – and so I usually managed to suppress any HIV worries with the thought that at least I wasn't harming anyone else.

Once we had decided to have a baby all hell broke loose. My wife had never felt herself at any risk, but all I could think of as I went to bed each night was that if I was HIV positive and we had unprotected sex then I was putting both my wife and any future baby in jeopardy. To try to make myself feel better, I would work out the statistical probability of my being HIV positive. I would guesstimate both the risk factor attached to each of my sexual encounters – drug addict, casual user, might have slept with a bisexual man, etc. – and the likely incidence of female infection in the years in question, and depending on my mood and level of anxiety the odds would come out anywhere between evens and a million to one. Yet I never did feel better, because no matter how hard I tried I couldn't eliminate the risk entirely. Whichever way I looked at it, someone somewhere who had lived my kind of life was going to get unlucky – so why shouldn't that someone be me?

As if on cue, my body started to play up. I would wake up at 3 a.m. soaked in sweat and, as anyone for whom *Black's Medical Dictionary* is essential bedtime reading will tell you, night sweats are one of the first signs of full-blown Aids. At first my wife had been solicitous about me. I naturally assumed that she had been impressed by my

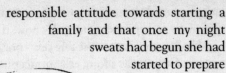

responsible attitude towards starting a family and that once my night sweats had begun she had started to prepare herself to look after a man with only a few more years to live. After a short while I realized that her concern wasn't for my physical state; she actually thought I was going mad.

There's something incredibly irritating about the way people treat you when they think you're bonkers. They start talking to you as if you were a five-year-old. Luckily, with my wife, compassion fatigue tends to set in rather quickly and it wasn't long before her attempts at sympathy gave way to a more manageable annoyance.

'You don't have Aids,' she said sweetly one morning. 'You're having panic attacks, for fuck's sake. But if you're so concerned about it, why don't you go and have the sodding test? Since you're behaving as if you've got Aids, life can't get any worse if it turns out you are positive.'

Up till now I had been reluctant to have the test because I didn't think I could bear the agonies of waiting for the result. I wasn't too optimistic about my chances but I didn't want to have my last shred of hope ripped away. But what my wife had just said made perfect sense: I was in a no-lose situation. If by some faint chance I was in the clear then I need no longer worry, and if the result came up positive I would at least have the pleasure of being able to say, 'I told you so.'

One last call to the Aids Helpline in a futile attempt to get myself off the hook, and we were off to the clinic. It was a good half-hour's drive and I tried to fill the time appropriately. I told my wife that I loved her very much, and that it would be all right by me if she remarried after I was gone, providing she left a suitable period for mourning. Curiously, my wife didn't respond to the gravity of the situation. Her only comment was, 'The sooner this is over the better.'

One syringe full of blood and an hour's nervous pacing around the park and we were back for the result. Negative. I ask, 'What's the likelihood of a false reading?', the wife says, 'Shut up,' and we're out of there.

Unbelievable. I'm going to be OK. I can be a daddy. Oh thank you, God, I'll never switch off *Songs of Praise* again.

'Don't you ever do that to me again,' my wife said forcefully on the way home. 'I told you there was nothing wrong with you.'

'Well, if the night sweats weren't anything to do with Aids, do you think they might have been leukaemia?'

SEX

Sex is supposed to be the fun part of having a baby. The only trouble is I've often found that sex isn't much fun. Perhaps I should make myself clear. I've got no problems with the anticipation of having sex and the warm heady glow that comes after you've negotiated it successfully; it's the actual doing it that causes me grief. I know we're supposed to be living in Cosmoland where we're all sexual athletes and the world is one big shagathon, but I still find myself worrying from time to time whether I'm doing OK.

Will I come too soon? Have I got any spots on my back? Will I stay hard? Am I big enough? Are my flabby bits misbehaving? Is she doing a Meg Ryan? These are just some of the thoughts that regularly enter my head. Now my wife and I both know that the number one rule of any successful relationship is not to trash the other person's sexual performance, so I've never found any reassurance about these things to be particularly reassuring.

Despite these anxieties I've persevered at sex over the years and, even though I say so myself, I think I've had my fair share of triumphant moments. I've even done it when I'm not pissed or stoned. Yet when it came to having sex to make a baby I found I was a novice all over again.

It wasn't the contraception, or lack of it, that was the problem. It was the prospect of failure. During the seventies and early eighties I had been decidedly casual about contraception. As a spotty adolescent I had become somewhat fixated on condoms – or 'johnnies' as we used to call them. I had convinced myself that ownership of a packet of three would mark me out as an adult and thereby greatly increase my chances of a genuine sexual encounter. The only obstacle was buying them. In the days before condoms were laid out next to the sweets at the chemist you actually had to ask for them. I gave all the local chemists a wide berth – women shop assistants and too many customers – and headed off for an anonymous barber's shop hidden away in a side street. 'A packet of Durex, please,' I said nervously. The barber peered over his half-rim glasses and gave me such a  look of contempt, as if to say, 'No one would ever dream of fucking you, sonny,' that for years I had only to think of a condom to feel sexually humiliated.

So condoms were out of the question, and if I met a woman and it looked like we were going to end up in bed together I wouldn't risk dampening her passion by mentioning contraception before she did. If nothing was said, I'd wait until we shared a post-coital cigarette and discharge my responsibilities by asking, 'You are on the pill, aren't you?' Even when I embarked on a proper relationship it was always my partner who took the lead on contraception. Mind you, if I had been a girl going out with me, I think I would have done the same thing.

Throughout these periods of lax contraception I never once got a girlfriend pregnant. For many years I was unbearably self-congratulatory about this. It's not often I get to take the moral high ground and, when a number of friends got their partner pregnant by mistake, there was a certain smugness in seeing myself as a thoughtful, caring kind of guy. Once I was at liberty to get my wife pregnant I saw things rather differently. What was wrong with me? Why hadn't I got anyone pregnant? As far as I remembered every woman I had been out with had either had an abortion before she met me or had gone on to produce armies of children within minutes of leaving me. So there was nothing wrong with any of my partners and, given that there was no reason to believe that any of them had changed their contraceptive habits, the clear inference was that I wasn't up to it.

If this wasn't pressure enough, to get the true vision of hell I had only to look at what had happened to

various couples I knew who had failed to conceive after six months or so of trying. Their lives were dominated by the woman's monthly cycle, and at key moments, which were often planned weeks in advance, they shagged till they dropped. The routine would be: wake up, shag, go to work, meet partner in town at lunchtime and try to find somewhere for a quick five-minute shag, go back to work, come home, shag, watch TV, shag, pass out exhausted. Repeat till pregnant. Now, the idea of having a woman who is available for sex – sometimes even demanding it – at any time of the day or night might sound like any man's wet dream, but not when it's under these circumstances. There's nothing arousing or flattering about being treated as a sperm machine. One friend was told by his wife: 'I don't care if you have to think of Michelle Pfeiffer to do it, as long as you do it.' Quite apart from the fact that he was probably thinking about Michelle Pfeiffer anyway, this begged a serious question. Just who the hell was she thinking of? Too much of this sort of sex is enough to make anyone celibate.

Faced with all this I found that I was getting rather envious of those friends who had got their partners pregnant by accident and had become fathers by default. Losing control of your life in one disastrous emission seemed a small price to pay for not having to worry about whether you can do it. Besides which, while I would have only myself to blame if fatherhood didn't come up to scratch, these men would have licence to moan to their heart's content. Strangely, the men I know who have had the least conscious participation in their children's conception have turned out to be the most opinionated about the way they should be brought up. I've no idea why this should be so, but I hope it's because they feel guilty. I couldn't bear them to get off scot-free.

To cope with the tension of committed sex – or, as David Coleman might say, 110 per cent sex – I devised a brilliant plan: procrastination. My wife took little per-suading to become a willing accomplice, and together we announced to our friends that we would be trying for a child in eight months' time. The main purpose of this was to fool ourselves. It meant that we could have any number of practice shags free from any pressure. If my wife got pregnant we could pass it off with a self-satisfied, 'Got a bit carried away. Couldn't wait a moment longer,' and if she didn't then everything was going to schedule.

Inevitably my wife didn't get pregnant this way. We extended the eight months to ten – pressure of work, very inconvenient to get up the duff just now – and still nothing happened. We were forced to admit to ourselves that we were actively trying for a baby. Unwelcome side-effects immediately manifested themselves. I found myself priapic only at moments when conception was biologically impossible and developed headaches on all other occasions. Even so, a magnificent Blitz spirit took over and we did manage to do it from time to time. I still count those shags among my finest achievements.

THE TEST

'I'm meeting Patty after work so I'll be late back tonight. Oh, and by the way, I'm three or four days late with my period.'

Now, if my wife had made a big deal about this last piece of news I probably wouldn't have given it much thought, for, as a general rule, the more she goes on about something the less important it is. The offhandedness of her delivery put me on red alert.

'So, you think you're pregnant?'

'Mmm. I dunno. Maybe.'

'Well, let's buy a kit and find out.'

'Nah. It's still early days. Let's give it a week and if I still haven't come on, we'll do it then.'

My wife's relaxed approach was beginning to get on my nerves. After a few months of studying her cycle we both knew that she tended to be as regular as clockwork, and I understood her  well enough to know that if she said she was three or four days late it probably meant that the real figure was more like a week.

'No, let's do it now. It's not as though waiting will make any difference to the result.'

'No.'

Even then I could see that the writing was on the wall. What had started off as a joint venture, in which we were to share the joys of parenthood together, was rapidly turning into her pregnancy. However, as there was a fair possibility that I'd already missed at least one per cent of my baby's womb-time development, I was damned if I was going to miss much more. Throughout the course of the day I bombarded her with calls at work. I knew she would be far too embarrassed to ask the switchboard not to put her husband through and in the end I ground a compromise out of her to do the test in two days' time.

I still don't think my wife is fully aware of what those forty-eight hours cost me. There I was on the brink of being able to hold my head high in all male company and of being taken seriously by my parents, and I was being made to wait for no apparent reason. Still, there are some things that you just can't make a woman do, and taking a pregnancy test is one of them. Eventually the morning of the test arrived. I had contemplated offering to go to the loo with her to check she was doing everything properly, but something told me this wouldn't be a popular suggestion, and so I decided to play her at her own game.

'I'm just off to the loo now,' she said.

'Fine. Can you bring me the newspaper on your way back?'

Unfortunately my wife is a far more skilful politician than me. Five minutes later she came back, flung me the paper, and hopped into bed without saying a word. I picked up the paper and tried to take in the headlines, but the knowledge that she had the information was

22

unbearable. Within thirty seconds I had cracked.

'Well?'

'Well, what?'

This could have gone on for ever.

'Well – are you pregnant?'

'Oh, yeah.'

There's something about getting such wonderful news that makes you forget how irritated you are with the other person, and we flung our arms around each other. A long chorus of I love yous and Thank yous and I knew its and I never doubted for a moment we'd be able to do its followed, and then I reached for the telephone.

'Who are you ringing?'

'My mum and dad, Liz, Katy, Tom and Debby, Rod and Patty, Alex and Elena, Ricky, Barney and Tors, Jane and Stephen, and Peter and Jenny.'

'Well, I don't want you to.'

'Why not?'

'Because I want some time to get used to the idea.'

Christ, she had had half an hour, how much longer could she want?

'I'd like to wait for three months or so. If I'm going to miscarry it's likely to happen in the first twelve weeks, and I'd like to know that everything is probably going to be OK before I start telling people.'

So that was that. I'd just received the best news of my life and I was subject to a long-term gagging order. There were all those people out there who would either be very pleased for us, or, better still, immensely envious, and I couldn't tell them. For the next three months I would have to try to carry on as normal, knowing that the outside world still saw me as the man who couldn't do it. Somehow or other I managed to keep my mouth shut. Occasionally I would drop a few highly veiled references into conversations – more as a way of showing my wife that I wasn't completely controllable, rather than as a conscious attempt to break the *omertà* – but no one ever decoded them. Or if they did they kept stumm about it.

Typically, the lifting of reporting restrictions produced a profound sense of anti-climax. I felt like a government official releasing a thirty-year-old secret; the news is supposed to be a dramatic revelation but you know that you're telling everyone only because you no longer give a toss who finds out. In my own mind I had been a dad-to-be for quite some time, and while there was a moment's pleasure in catching people by surprise, it was hard to remain suitably enthusiastic. Friends would say, 'Let's celebrate,' and I would just think, 'Why?'

To be fair, it wasn't just the thought of being robbed of my moment of glory that was depressing me; I was also starting to wonder whether the baby was mine. My wife had no track record of serial infidelity – or none that I knew about – but whereas she could be absolutely certain the baby was hers, I would never know for sure it was mine. I'd always considered myself to be a fairly trusting bloke; I'd allowed my wife to go out without a chaperon and had never employed a private detective to check up on her at work. But now I regretted it. She could have been having it off with somebody else for years for all I knew.

A suspected infidelity, especially one with no evidence, isn't the easiest subject to broach with your wife, and so I tried to think of ways of proving my paternity that didn't involve her. The best that I could come up with was DNA testing after the baby was born. But even this didn't seem conclusive. What if it was the biochemist who was the father and he deliberately skewed the results? Even if I got an honest result, what would that prove? DNA fingerprinting isn't an exact science and could only give the likelihood of my being the father. Odds of 7,000,000–1 against anyone else being the father might be good enough for a court to settle a paternity suit, but they wouldn't be good enough for me. By my very simple maths that meant there would be at least three other men in Britain alone  who could be the father. And then there was the rest of the world to consider. Perhaps there was just one massively endowed man – The Great Impregnator – to whom every woman went when she wanted to have a baby, and men had been duped all along?

In time I realized that I would never know and that my doubts would always remain. It was then that I understood why so many men had seemed so pleased when I told them I was going to be a dad.

WHOSE LIFE IS IT ANYWAY?

Possession may be nine-tenths of the law as far as most things are concerned, but with a foetus it's everything. And I didn't have it. I still think it was only this knowledge that kept my wife's spirits up throughout the nine months of her pregnancy.

'I do feel very sorry for you,' she would say. 'It must be difficult for you to feel any empathy with the baby, whereas I feel that I already have quite an intense relationship.'

Now you can take that as a genuine expression of sympathy if you like, but I knew better. What she was really saying was, 'I've got a massive head start on you. The baby will love me much, much more than you when it's born, and frankly I don't think you'll ever catch up.' And the thing is, she was right. I would try to rectify the situation by pressing my head up against my wife's tummy and saying, 'It's Daddy here. I know that life's a bit dull inside Mummy but everything's going to be just great once you're out,' but I knew that I was clutching at straws. In any case, access to this sort of conversation was severely restricted by you-know-who.

Women often complain of how out of control they feel during pregnancy, which only goes to show that they've never bothered to think about how men feel. I tried hard to continue to relate to my wife as an adult independent woman, but the fact is I saw her more and more as the physical receptacle for our child – much in the way that the Big Daddy Alien must have viewed John Hurt. These were  dangerous waters. I knew that the thought police would be down on me in seconds if I dared utter a word of this, and I spent a lot of time wondering how I was going to deal with it. I settled for trying to monitor every moment of my wife's existence; I could pretend to be endlessly concerned for her well-being while keeping a beady eye on what was happening to the baby.

This was easier said than done.

'What a day. I could murder a beer. Will you get me one?'

'Are you sure you wouldn't rather have a mineral water?'

'No. I want a bloody beer and stop annoying me.'

I'd no intention of stopping.

'Will a low-alcohol one do?'

'No.'

At which point I would go and get her half a glass of Beck's.

This might look like rather feeble resistance on my part, but it was hard to be too dogmatic because even I could see that her entire pregnancy wasn't being spent in a drunken stupor. I'd read the literature on alcohol during pregnancy and, while I was certain that these

books had been written by people who were prone to the odd tipple, it did seem as though a beer every three or four days couldn't do much harm. Even so I always did wonder exactly how much alcohol it takes to render a two-centimetre foetus completely unconscious, and I maintained my vigil right till the end of the pregnancy – just in case things ever looked like getting out of hand.

Keeping track of my wife's food intake was relatively easy. I could study the list of ingredients and sling out anything that reeked of unpleasant colourings or carcinogenic additives. Where things really fell apart was at a friend's party. My wife had been happy to call herself a non-smoker for some years, but the moment we arrived she made a bee-line for the nearest person holding a cigarette, regardless of whether she liked or even knew him. She then hovered around hopefully, nodding her head at whatever the person was droning on about. Before long a snout was politely offered and my wife duly grabbed it: 'I know I shouldn't, but I just can't resist. Still, one won't hurt, will it?'

This was clearly a direct challenge. My wife was gambling that the weight of numbers would stop me from making a scene. I tried coughing very loudly, but no one paid much notice. I upped the stakes.

'At what stage do the lungs form?' I shouted.

A nervous silence followed, and then the other guests

began to congregate around my wife to offer her their condolences. Anyone would have thought it was me who was trying to kill our child, for God's sake. I drew the line at ripping the cigarette out of her mouth, and so I was forced to let her smoke and gloat in peace. I don't regret what I did, though; at least we weren't invited to any more parties.

My wife and I might not have been able to agree on some of her more dubious personal habits, but we were united in some things. For instance, we both wanted to know exactly what was going on with our baby at all times. When my wife's pregnancy had first been  confirmed we'd rushed out and bought a whole library of books on childbirth. However, I soon had to stop reading them because they were far too depressing. Every page I turned to alluded to some potential disaster. I had enough sense to recognize that this was probably an editorial ploy to frighten the reader into staying awake through what was otherwise the dreariest, most sanctimonious prose imaginable, but, even so, it made me think. Having a baby was a very dangerous occupation.

I realized that while there were some conditions nobody could detect, there were others that one most definitely could. And my wife and I wanted to know if our baby had them. Our main worry was Down's syndrome, as my wife was of an age where this was a realistic possibility. The only sure-fire way to find out was to have an amniocentesis, but my wife was reluctant to do this. Quite apart from the risk of miscarriage, the idea of having a six-inch needle jabbed into her stomach made her rather queasy. When I thought of our baby waking up from a twelve-hour kip to find a stainless-steel spike inches from its nose, I tended to agree.

It was then that the pregnancy grapevine took over and we got to hear of the Harris Birthright Trust. The trust had pioneered a technique of assessing the probability of Down's from an ultrasound scan, so that it was only if you got a bad result that you really needed an amnio. It seemed too good to be true, but as even the most agnostic of our friends talked about the place in hallowed terms, we decided to go along.

On arrival, it was obvious that we weren't the only people to have heard of the place. The corridor was teeming with expectant couples and a sign showed that appointments were running two hours late. Too much time to think is bad for the psyche. All Down's statistics are based on probabilities, and I found myself counting the number of pregnant mums. By my reckoning it was likely that someone in the queue was going to be unfortunate. So who was it? I tried studying the faces of people as they were leaving but everyone remained steadfastly impassive, determined not to give anything away. I tried another tack. Suppose two people before us got bad news. Would that make us twice as likely to be OK?

Just as I was grappling with this conundrum we were called through into a darkened room. My wife was made to lie down, her tummy was smeared with goo and, as if by magic, our baby appeared on screen. Up to this point most of my feelings and thoughts towards the baby had veered to the abstract, but I have to confess that I'd always rather assumed it would be a boy. This may have been partly a deep-rooted chauvinism, but I'd never been that big on the 'son and heir' stuff, and I'm inclined to think that it had more to do with my inability to imagine a baby that was different to me. As soon as I saw the outline of the baby, I instinctively knew she was a girl. And I fell in love with her on the spot. There she was lying down, with her legs crossed, sucking her thumb, in exactly the same position as my wife had been when we first met.

Within ten minutes the foetal measurements were complete and the results were looking good. There was only a 1 in 500 chance that our baby had Down's. This wasn't quite the 100 per cent all-clear that I would have liked, but seeing that the risk of a miscarriage after an amnio was now five times higher than that of finding anything wrong, they were odds I was prepared to accept. After all, I didn't want to have to go through all that reproductive sex again.

MY LIFE AS A DOG

'Things are going to be a bit tight when the baby's born. You'll have to try to earn a bit more.'

Great. It was our baby, but it was me who was going to have to earn more.

'Oh, no problem. I'll just ring up my editors and tell them that my wife's up the duff and I need to be paid more. I'm sure they'll be thrilled to add a few noughts to the cheques.'

'I just meant that if you were a little more organized you could probably get a lot more done.'

We were now moving on to familiar territory. My wife was on a monthly salary. This meant that she could spend half her time hanging around the coffee machine and still consider herself fantastically busy. I was self-employed. This meant that a five-minute personal phone call was a profligate waste of potential earning time.

'You're right. If I got up at half-past five I could probably fit in a bit of shelf stacking at Sainsbury's, and they're always advertising for night security guards and mini-cab drivers. Who knows? I might even be able to manage the odd half-hour with you and the baby providing I don't bother to sleep.'

'Stop being so bloody touchy.'

It was hard not to be touchy because ever since we had met my wife had earned more than me. At first it had seemed vaguely alternative to be a kept man, but once I had got something I could identify as a life, I had found my PC liberalism eroding. I knew that I should be able to accept the situation and talk knowingly of role reversal, but I just couldn't bring myself to grow the beard, wear the dungarees and move to Camden.

It's not that I minded my wife earning a lot of money, because there were undeniably one or two advantages. Salesmen would automatically assume that it was me who had come in to buy the new car. The little woman would be given a nice cup of tea while I got the test drive and macho sales spiel. I actually found the torque talk completely baffling but it was worth listening just to see my wife get angry. Which reminds me – I really ought to let her drive the car from time to time.

The heart of the problem was that I thought I should be earning more than her – not because I needed to, but as a matter of principle. Over the years I had come up with various ways to cope with the income disparity. The most satisfactory was to attack her work. This would have been a great deal easier if she had had some dull City job where she was paid a fortune for swindling punters by moving numbers from one side of the computer screen to the other. As it was, her work was almost interesting – some might even have said creative – and so my sniping had to be much less direct. My aim was to keep up a supportive façade while continually under-mining her. Whenever she got home I would make a big deal of asking about her day, but always referring to her meetings as 'get-togethers' and business trips as 'outings'. This was designed to make her realize that her daily routine was essentially a series of incredibly trivial, not to say menial, tasks, and that, by definition, she was grossly overpaid.

However, with the imminent arrival of a baby, these tactics were proving markedly less effective.

'It's all very well for you. You'll still be getting paid even when you're in labour. Who's going to pay me to be there at the birth?'

'Look, I don't want to make a big song and dance about it. I think your work's going very well. I just wanted to point out that things are bound to change a bit. Oh, and while you're up, get me another drink, will you?'

From where I was standing, things already had changed. And not for the better. The rest of my adult life

 was to be spent as a donkey, fetching and carrying and making sure that my wife and child had everything they needed to guarantee them a hassle-free

existence. The future had become blindingly clear. 'I think that she should have piano lessons.' 'But I'm already working my butt off to pay for the gym classes.' 'If you think you're overdoing it, perhaps you should up the life insurance.'

When I'd first considered what might be involved in becoming a dad, the idea of giving up some of the fun parts of my life-style hadn't seemed too threatening. So I might have to miss my Saturday morning game of footie? Not too many worries there. I'd got a bit fed up with all those much younger players running rings round me anyway. So I would no longer be able to jack in my job for six months to go travelling. Who cared? I liked what I was doing and in any case there was nowhere I was desperately keen to go. No more spur-of-the-moment trips to the pub? No problem. There was always the off-licence. As for those Sunday morning lie-ins, my insomnia took care of them.

What I had failed to realize was that along with my loss of independence would come a complete loss of identity. From now on I would no longer be a person. I would be a daddy instead. And traditionally daddies got a very raw  deal. Mummies would get the good stuff, the concern – 'You're looking very tired' – and the four months' holiday a.k.a. maternity leave, while the best that a daddy could hope for was to be ignored. The only time anyone ever bothered to find out how a daddy was feeling was when they asked him if he was well enough to sign the cheque.

Now that the baby was a fait accompli I was beginning to have second thoughts about the whole thing. Was it really worth subjecting myself to a lifetime of relentless, thankless slavery? What would be my reward for the never-ending cycle of nappy changing and getting up in the night? If I was lucky – very lucky – it would be to find one day that my child had turned into a grumpy dope-smoking teenager, whose only words to me would be, 'You really messed me up.'

NO SEX

Many books say that women are at their most radiant during pregnancy. These must have been written either by women or by perverts. Sex is difficult enough at the best of times without having a pregnancy to contend with. You might just be able to get away with it in the early stages when you can forget for a moment that there is another person growing inside your partner, but once the visible signs are there – not a chance.

Late one night, when my wife was about six months pregnant, we were lying in bed reading when she turned to me and said, 'Do you still fancy me?'

My wife has an endearing habit of introducing heavyweight conversations just when I want to go to sleep. She hopes that she's going to catch me off guard, and even if she doesn't, she knows that she's sure to ruin my night's sleep.

'Yes, of course I do.'

I wasn't as dozy as all that.

'Then why haven't you wanted to make love to me recently?'

Yes, I was.

'I have.'

'Don't lie. You haven't.'

'I have wanted to. I just haven't been able to.'

I was wide awake by now and thinking fast. It was time to switch the focus.

'In any case, I haven't noticed you making any wild passes at me in the last few months.'

'That's not the point.'

But it was the point, and we both knew it. She couldn't handle getting down to the nitty-gritty any more than me. We both liked the idea of having sex, but we were so alarmed about what was happening to her body that neither of us was really capable of doing anything about it.

The trouble was that we both somehow felt that we ought to be doing something about it. All the descriptions of sex during pregnancy that I had come across in the parenting books had been couched in terms of 'beautiful' and 'natural'. To add weight to this thesis they helpfully included illustrations of people looking 'beautiful' and 'natural' as they did it. These showed a couple – far younger than my wife and I, incidentally – blissfully conjoined with the support of various items of household paraphernalia, such as cushions, chairs and tables. It goes without saying that neither party had a hair out of place nor showed any signs of physical exertion in maintaining positions of immense technical difficulty. You can bet your life that if the book had ever come out in audio-visual format, the drawings would have been accompanied by contented sighs, rather than cries of, 'I can't breathe,' 'My back hurts,' or 'Get your hands off me, you filthy bastard.'

I'm all for being liberal about sex, but I think you can

go too far. It was clear that the only reason the sections on sex during pregnancy had been included was to make a few sexual deviants, who couldn't keep their hands off each another for more than a few days, feel better about themselves. To me there was nothing natural or beautiful about having sex while my wife was noticeably pregnant.

To start with, her body now looked nothing like the one to which I'd first been attracted. Almost by the day, it seemed, her breasts were getting larger and larger. I suppose some men might look on this as an advantage, but I had always rather liked my wife's breasts the way they were. What had once been held in delicate French lace were now enveloped in yards of reinforced off-white cotton. This was a bra designed with one thing in mind – to keep men out – and it served as a potent symbol that there was shortly to be a change of use. Breasts that had previously existed purely as a pleasure zone for me and, I like to think, my wife were turning into a food source for the baby. And it's hard to feel too sexually aroused when you're competing for space with your child.

Of course the most distinctive change to my wife's body was around the waistline. In many ways, my wife found this more disturbing than me, but then if it had been me who had lost sight of my own toes I would probably have felt the same way as her. The fact is that I found it rather reassuring to watch her get bigger, as it was one of the few signs available to me that the pregnancy was progressing normally. This was undoubtedly

made easier by my never having identified the tummy as an erogenous location. Having little imagination can sometimes be a great asset. There was a downside to the tumescence, though. As the baby got bigger and bigger, my mind became concentrated on how it was going to get out. Predictably, this turned an area of sexual mystery into a straightforward business development district. There was no getting away from it; whichever way I looked, nature was telling me that sex was out of the question. I was not wanted on voyage.

I considered taking inordinate amounts of Prozac to help me come to terms with this, but it seemed a bit pointless. Even if I could learn to deal with the physical attributes of pregnancy, there wasn't a drug invented that could offset the psychological complications. Having sex with a pregnant woman was so loaded with hideous Freudian scenarios that it was guaranteed to reduce any normal, well-adjusted man to impotence. The question was: if I went to bed with my wife, just who would I be having sex with?

My wife was very obviously turning into a mummy. Every time I looked at her I thought of mummies, and

often, in particular, of my own mother. People say that every man marries his mother. This may well be so, but I had no desire to sleep with mine. Having sex with your mother may be the apotheosis of a therapist's experience – the unconscious desire made conscious – but I simply wasn't enlightened enough for that. Besides which, my mum has had grey hair as long as I can remember. This isn't just a passing ageist comment, but a genuine expression of guilt. My sisters always used to joke, 'John turned Mum grey,' but it was obvious from my mum's expression that she didn't think it at all funny because in her mind it was true. So, sleeping with my pregnant wife was laden with anxiety. I just couldn't have handled it if she had turned grey, too.

Worse still was the thought that I would be having sex with my baby. Aside from the blatant connotations of child abuse, I was concerned about how the foetus would interpret my wife and me having sex. The proximity to my dick would at the very least have been highly disruptive, and could even have made it fearful for its safety. It was possible that the baby would have felt unwanted. It might have thought that, as we were continuing to have sex after conception, we either didn't know it was inside or that we didn't care and were trying to replace it with another baby.

Maternity professionals often suggest having sex as a way of inducing an overdue baby. This is because they have seen so many pregnancies that childbirth has become a routine conveyor-belt activity. Think about it. If you were a baby which would you prefer? Being nudged and poked and jigged about or being left to come out when you were ready? Having sex to bring on a baby is no better than a property speculator sending in the heavies to clear out unwanted tenants – brutal and sadistic.

The good thing about a pregnancy is that it doesn't last for ever. So while having sex when my wife was pregnant was something I never fully came to terms with, I always knew it was one of the few problems that would respond to inertia. In the end, I settled for talking about it a lot. That way I could always tell myself that if it wasn't for the baby I would be constantly at it.

WHAT IS IT?

'Everything's absolutely fine.'

We were back at the hospital for another scan even though we'd already been told that our baby didn't have spina bifida and all its vital organs were working. Under normal circumstances my first response would have been, 'Are you sure?' but just then I'd got a far more pressing question.

'Can you tell us what sex the baby is?'

Although I'd had a strong feeling that our baby was a girl when we'd gone for the first scan, it had been too early for any conclusive proof.

'Are you sure you want to know? Many parents prefer it to be a surprise.'

I know that, you stupid old bastard, now just get on with it.

'Yes, we're sure.'

'Well, she looks very like a girl to me.'

Yes. This was fantastic news. Not because I'd had a particular preference for a girl, but because it meant that I'd been right.

'I knew it.'

I didn't want to sound too triumphant, but it was important to remind my wife who had been the first person to identify the sex correctly. The baby might be growing away inside her, but it was me who had the closer connection with it.

All this was useful point-scoring; it was also, unfortunately, complete bullshit. In the intervening weeks before the second scan I'd kept up an unwavering campaign of 'It's definitely a girl' only because there seemed no reason not to. If it turned out I was right I could crow about it and make all sorts of extravagant claims for my intuitive fathering abilities, while if I was wrong no one would give a monkey's anyway. The reality was that ever since that first scan I'd had serious doubts about my predictive powers. In fact, things had got so bad that I was struggling even to think of the baby as human. To me it was just a sort of blob. And with these thoughts came an overwhelming sense of failure. My initial outpourings of love had slowed to a trickle, and now my primary emotion was bewilderment. Where were all those marvellous paternal feelings I was supposed to have?

One weekend, when my wife was about twenty-four weeks pregnant, I was busy hunting for the bacon counter that Sainsbury's had moved for my added convenience, when I was rammed in the back of the legs by another shopping trolley.

'Watch where you're going.'

This was my standard response to any supermarket accident, and the words were out of my mouth before I'd even bothered to turn round to see who had hit me. From past experience I expected the culprit to be either some steroid-riddled body builder who was finding it difficult to squeeze his way down the aisles or an out-of-control teenager who was terrified that any of his mates would catch him out shopping with his parents. I was shocked to find that it was a young mum with a six-month-old baby draped round her neck and a two-year-old trying to escape from her trolley. Abusing young women in public instantly marks you out as a homicidal maniac and, to save myself from a lynching, I hastily mumbled an apology.

Later on, as I was dawdling in front of the ice-cream fridges, I realized why I had found the incident so disturbing. It wasn't because I had lost my temper, but because I wasn't really very sorry. There I was, a daddy-to-be, and I couldn't even make allowances for a mother and her two infants.

Before my wife had got pregnant, I had been completely indifferent to children. To be fair, when friends had babies I would always trot off to the hospital to pay my respects, and I would try to make appreciative remarks, such as, 'It looks all right.' But my heart was never in it, because I knew that from then on my relationship with my friends was as good as over. They would never go out again, their only topic of conversation would be their children, and they would socialize only with other people with children.

Somehow I'd imagined that having my own child would mystically change things but, even with my wife six months gone, it was clear there was a world of difference between wanting a child and loving it.

Knowing that we were going to have a girl helped a bit, because it meant that the baby became slightly more humanoid and could even have a name. Many couples find the business of naming their children hopelessly traumatic, but we found it remarkably easy. We eliminated the names of everyone we knew – especially family – on the grounds that we didn't want to lumber the baby with any offensive associations, and chose the only other one we liked. And so the blob became Jo.

Even with a name, it wasn't that easy relating to Jo.

 For one thing she was hardly ever there. My wife would get up, bolt down some breakfast, and then selfishly take the baby to work with her. And that would be that until seven in the evening.

Whenever I moaned about this, my wife would say, 'Believe me, I wish it was you who was having the bloody baby.' Now I'd always looked on the impossibility of getting pregnant as one of the highlights of being male, but it looks pretty poor to admit that you've deliberately got your wife into a condition you would never consider for yourself, and so I'd always reply, 'So do I.' Which, in part, was true. I was jealous of her closeness to Jo. Even if my wife had no more clue than I did about what Jo was actually like, she still had a very physical link to her.

As ever, my wife showed a natural flair for exploiting a situation.

'Ow. Jo's kicking hard tonight. Come and have a feel.'

I would leap up and place my hand firmly on her

46

stomach. Whereupon precisely nothing would happen.

'It's funny how she always stops when you put your hand there. Maybe it quietens her down.'

Or maybe she was never moving in the first place. Or maybe she knew that mine were the hands of a child-hater, and she was cowering in terror.

I tried repeating the mantra 'Daddy loves you' as I did the laying on of hands, but even then I never got any response. Perhaps Jo wasn't sure if I was telling the truth. I thought that I loved her, but I had nothing to judge it against. I'd never had a love affair with someone I couldn't see,  touch or hear before. There was something to be said for all this uncertainty, though. It wasn't me who was going to get post-natal depression.

BABY SCHOOL

Mercifully, all my problems were about to be solved. I was going to be taught how to be the perfect daddy.

One evening my wife returned home from work to announce that she had booked us both up for ante-natal classes.

'What the hell are they?'

'Come on, everyone's heard of them.'

Everyone who's white, middle class and pregnant, that is.

'So tell me, then.'

'We turn up an evening a week over the last couple of months of the pregnancy, and someone shows us what to do in labour and how to look after the baby.'

I was tempted to ask what any of that had got to do with me, but, with the birth becoming imminent, my wife was quickly losing her sense of humour. My PC credentials, such as they were, had to be both seen and heard.

'That sounds like a good idea.'

Sycophantic enough?

It sounded desperate. I wasn't averse to the idea of picking up a few handy hints on being a daddy, but I had a sneaking feeling that the classes were all going to be about motherhood. I could almost guarantee that the person in charge would be a woman, and that after spending an hour and twenty-five minutes crapping on about breast-feeding, she would fill the last five minutes with, 'And we mustn't forget the fathers. They're very important too.' And it would be obvious that she meant exactly the opposite. Still, I'd promised to be supportive and at the worst the classes would provide me with a checklist so I'd know when my wife was doing it wrong.

We arrived at the appointed hour for our first lesson, and were met at the door of an expensive-looking house by a glamorous middle-aged woman.

'Hi, I'm Judy. Come in.'

Judy was wearing a pale yellow velveteen track suit which perfectly emphasized her slim, athletic body. She also had five children, all of whom were dotted around the various rooms of their enormous home, engaged in acts of suitable creativity. The whole house was a shrine to family values, and Judy's welcoming smile seemed to be saying, 'Just listen to me, and all this can be yours, too.'

After the obligatory ten minutes of small-talk, Judy decided it was time to get things going.

'I think we should go round the room one by one and introduce ourselves and say a little bit about how we're feeling.'

'I'm Justin, and I'm very excited about becoming a dad.'

'I'm Ruth. I'm feeling a little tired but otherwise everything's fine.'

'I'm Nick, and I'm thrilled about it all.'

'I'm Emily, and I can't wait to have the baby.'

'I'm John. I'm shit-scared, and there are times when I think we've made a ghastly mistake.'

Silence.

'Er, thank you for sharing that with us, John. It's good to be reminded that parenthood can bring up some difficult feelings. Now, where were we?'

From that moment on I always felt like a social pariah in the classes. Even to my wife. On the way home she had rounded on me and said, 'Don't ever embarrass me like that again.' Now I admit that I had got a little perverse enjoyment from my outburst, but it was hardly shock-jock tactics. If anything, I had understated how I really felt. Yet even a honed-down emotion, such as shit-scared, was too much. The rules of engagement for future classes were clearly defined. All feelings had to be sanitized. You could feel 'a bit upset' and things could be 'a little tricky', but desperate was out of the question. And above all, there was nothing – absolutely nothing – that couldn't be fixed.

Over the next few weeks we were taught how to give birth the proper way. This involved studying *The Lives of the Martyrs*. For Judy, there was no pain that was unendurable, and the road to perfect motherhood was a drug-free delivery. Occasionally some of the women – most notably my wife – would ask her about epidurals, gas and air, and pethidine. Judy stopped short of dismissing these questions as Devil's talk, but her look of distress and the thirty seconds subsequently allotted to the discussion of these crimes against humanity told us exactly how she felt. Surprisingly, Judy's fundamentalist Christian

Science beliefs struck a chord with me. I'd been worrying about how I might feel when my wife was being offered hard drugs and I wasn't, and now I had something with which to bully her into refusing them.

Judy knew all about the weakness of the flesh, though, and we were given *Blue Peter*-style lessons in pain resistance. Take one plastic bucket and squat on it, take two tennis balls and roll them up and  down your back, spray water in your face and, hey presto, you won't feel a thing. If that didn't work there were breathing techniques and massage to consider. My wife quite fancied the massage option, but as I was already finding sex during pregnancy a nightmare, I categorically refused to give it a go while she was in labour. The pièce de résistance was relaxation training. Judy would darken the room, put on a tape, and expect us all to be as one with the universe. I suppose some people might be able to nod off to 'Richard Clayderman Murders Bach', but I'm not one of them, and I would find myself sitting there, stuck somewhere between laughter and irritation. It was like being taken back eighteen years to my college days when I would sit up half the night smoking joint after joint of third-rate Moroccan while some moron played the same dreary Steely Dan track over and over again.

As the classes progressed, a subversive solidarity emerged among the men as we became more and more marginalized. I reached the point where I could stop worrying how much more than me the other men were earning, but even so I never felt wholly comfortable with them. In the penultimate session, Judy had split the men and women into separate groups, and asked us both to compile a list of the things that were worrying us about having a baby. The men were sent downstairs to the kitchen. This was a bit of a result, because it meant that we could catch up with the England game on the radio. Fifteen minutes later we felt sufficiently guilty to start making a list.

After being trashed for having a feeling in the first class, I was reluctant to expose myself again, but no one was saying anything, and I thought that nobody would find my main anxiety the slightest bit controversial.

'I'm worried about the baby dying at birth.'

'You what?'

'You know, stillbirth, that kind of thing.'

'God. How neurotic can you get?'

I took it as read that no one else was concerned about their partner dying.

'Well, what kinds of things are you worried about then?'

'I dunno really. I haven't given it much thought. I'm not much looking forward to changing dirty nappies or getting woken up the whole time,' said Mark.

'Neither am I,' said Justin.

'Nor me,' said Nick.

And there we had it. Top of the men's list came changing nappies, next came lack of sleep, and then a whole string of items too trivial to mention. Without exception the other men refused to list my worries along with theirs, and the only compromise we could reach was to have a separate agenda called 'John's List'. This was not mindless bravado on their part; they lived in a world where everyone had perfect, happy, bouncing babies, and they expected no less for themselves. But it wasn't my world. The closer it  got to the birth, the more I thought about death. Birth and death were just two ends of the same spectrum, and often there was precious little between them.

It was the unswerving cheeriness of the ante-natal classes that did it for me. I felt bad about this because a lot of people evidently found them a great help, but I just knew that I wasn't cut out to be a professional parent. For the sake of my wife I promised to go to the odd reunion tea party, but I couldn't see myself hacking it for more than a year. So Jo wouldn't grow up to play in the park with the children of Justin and Ruth, and Nick and Emily, and Mark and Karen. Which is a bit sad, really. Because she would probably have found life a great deal easier if she had.

NEARLY READY

Early on in the pregnancy we'd been given a due date of 5 July. At the time I'd dismissed this as pure guesswork because I couldn't see how any doctor could possibly tell which was the crucial shag. With less than a month to go, there was nothing arbitrary about it: 5 July was the day that Jo would be born.

This wasn't due to any medical or astrological updates, but to anxiety pure and simple. In the last few months of my wife's pregnancy I had felt my life slipping faster and faster out of control, and I needed something concrete, something definite to hang on to. The birth date was all I could think of. And so the birth date it was. I would count down the weeks – ten, nine, eight and so on – and refuse to make arrangements for any dates after the fifth. If anyone remarked that the baby might be late, I would just ignore them.

'You must try to enjoy your last few weeks together before the baby's born,' said my mother. 'It really can be a very special time.'

I can't say that enjoyment was a major feature of the pre-birth weeks, but my mum was certainly right about it being a special time. Seldom had I been presented with so many neurotic opportunities all at once.

Before my wife became pregnant I had looked on childbirth as a perfectly ordinary life activity. Men went bald and women had babies. Enough said. As my wife grew progressively larger, I didn't feel so sanguine about it. I was finding it harder and  harder to reconcile the discrepancy between the size of the bump and the size of the aperture, and by the time she was eight months gone giving birth looked to be an anatomical impossibility.

Life was made a great deal easier by the knowledge that it wouldn't be me who was required to put nature to the test, but, even so, it was all very worrying. And you know what? At the very moment when I most wanted a lot of love and looking after, my wife had irritatingly come over all needy on me. Just because she was heavily pregnant I was now expected to be utterly supportive and to have no feelings whatsoever. So I couldn't even tell her how worried I was. How self-centred can you get? Who was going to take care of me, for God's sake?

Mind you, there were some worries that could never have been disclosed under any circumstances. I had this recurring fantasy that something was going to go wrong with the birth, and that the doctor would say to me, 'Well, Mr Crace, we can save either your wife or the baby. Which is it to be?' Imagine having to choose between being labelled a wife-killer or a child-killer. I quickly decided that it would have to be my wife who was reprieved, but the fact that I'd had to think about it at all made me feel enormously guilty every time I looked at her.

This played havoc with my TV viewing.

'There's nothing much on tonight. Do you mind if I watch the footie?'

'Jo gets all agitated whenever the sport comes on, and I get really uncomfortable. I think we'd better watch *Northern Exposure*.'

And I'm ashamed to say that I let her get away with it.

As a result of my morbid thoughts I had deliberated long and hard over which hospital would get the honour of delivering Jo. Most people have to make do with whichever is nearest, but, being thirty-five, my wife was regarded as a geriatric freak by the doctors, and we were offered the freedom of the health authority. Now, some might have gone for the newest or the one with the birthing pool, but I opted for the one with the best paediatric intensive care facilities. It may have been the dirtiest and the shabbiest and, thanks to the government, due to be shut down, but to me it was by far the safest.

In a bid further to improve the odds of a trouble-free delivery I started to plea-bargain with God. This was necessarily rather tricky as He and I didn't have a great track record together, and my church attendance was almost non-existent. I liked the idea of there being a God because life seemed inherently pointless without one, but my beliefs were founded on a bit of hope and a lot of doubt rather than anything so grand as faith. Still, that's where being brought up a Protestant helped. As a Catholic I would have been doomed, but in the Anglican Church my level of doubt marked me out as a potential spiritual giant.

'I tell you what, God, if I promise to go to church

more often and I transform our home into one fit for the princess, then you'll take care of the birth. OK?'

On a good day I'd interpret the silence as 'Yes' and on a bad day as 'No'.

Having made the deal I was then left wondering just how good the princess's home needed to be. It would be nice to say that my wife was a tower of strength in this, but quite  frankly she was worse than useless. As far as I knew women were supposed to get all broody and clean out cupboards, but my wife was having none of that. Her three weeks' maternity leave before the birth was the last bit of peace and quiet she was going to get for some time, and she was too busy putting her feet up to consider doing anything remotely energetic. So all the nesting got left to me. I figured that God wouldn't expect me to do all the girly things around the house, so I set about repainting the radiators and the skirting-boards and fixing the gutter that had leaked continuously for the past eighteen months.

It was the garden that got the full treatment, though. At the time we were living in the middle of one of the busiest one-way systems in London, and I had this vision of creating a little oasis of flowers and running water,  where my wife and I could sit with Jo and get on with a little gentle bonding. The flowers were easy, but running water meant digging a pond, and buying a liner and a pump. A day's hard graft and £120 later, the pond

was in business. Two days later there was a radio programme about the number of child drownings in garden ponds. Within hours the pond was history.

The final part of the equation was getting all the baby clobber. This was another exercise in guilt. Whenever I was toying with buying a cheaper model I would hear Jo saying, 'You tight bastard. I'm going to make your life hell if you get that one.' So I invariably bought the most expensive items I could afford. And when you're talking prams and cots and clothes and sterilizers and baby

alarms this comes to a hell of a lot of money. I only hoped the little darling would be grateful.

By the beginning of July my preparations were finally complete, but I was

far too tense to relax. My concentration span was completely shot so I couldn't get much work done; I would leave my desk every twenty minutes to check on something I'd checked twenty minutes previously. I consoled myself with the thought that with all I'd done, everything would be plain sailing once Jo was born. Just how deluded can you get?

HELLO STRANGER

'Well, where is she, then?'

It was just after lunch on 5 July and I was getting rather tetchy about Jo's non-appearance. My wife knew there was a deadline, and I couldn't help feeling that she was hanging on to her for as long as possible to prevent me from seeing her.

'Just give it a rest. Do you think I enjoy being like this?'

I'd been going on about Jo being born on 5 July for so long that even my wife had begun to believe it, and now that the day had arrived the waiting was killing us. I had woken at seven-thirty, checked that nothing was happening with my wife, and spent the rest of the morning trying to read the Sunday papers in front of the TV.

The afternoon had disappeared in much the same fashion, when shortly before supper my wife started to complain of feeling a bit odd.

'How odd?'

'I just feel funny.'

'Having a baby funny?'

'How would I know? I've never had one before.'

Oh ha ha.

'Do you think it's possible, though?'

'Maybe.'

All those ante-natal classes had been a great help.

I could tell that the conversation had gone as far as it was going to, and, in the interests of marital harmony, I decided not to mention the oddness again before she did. However, whenever I didn't think she was looking, I would stare at her to see if she looked any odder. The results were sadly inconclusive, and by the time we went to bed I was convinced that her condition was psychosomatic.

We'd been sitting reading in bed for about ten minutes when my wife announced that she was sitting in a damp patch.

'Have you wet yourself?'

Look, I know it wasn't the most tactful thing to say, but it was eleven forty-five at night, mild incontinence had been one of the less enchanting features of the last few weeks of the pregnancy, and I didn't want to get all worked up about nothing.

'No, I haven't.'

The lack of abuse and her thoughtful expression made me realize she was telling the truth.

'Well, have your waters broken, then?'

'I think they must have done.'

It was all a bit low-key really. When I'd first heard of 'waters breaking' I'd thought of spectacular torrents of holy water, and it was hard to reconcile the small stain on the right-hand side of the bed with Jo's first movements towards independence. Still, I wasn't going to complain. For one thing, it meant – yet again – that I'd got something right about Jo before my wife, and for another it meant that we could at last go to the hospital. Over the previous ten days, the sheer size of my wife's tummy and the idea of getting stuck in rush-hour traffic had led me to believe that she ought to spend the rest of her pregnancy in hospital, wired up to a foetal heart monitor. Always one to be difficult, my wife had expressed a desire to remain at home as long as possible.

'We'd better get off, then.'

'Steady on. The contractions haven't even started.'

'Remember what they said at the classes. Go to hospital as soon as the waters break.'

Got her. She'd never dare argue with St Judy.

'All right, then.'

I slung on some clothes, picked up a book and a radio for the cricket – well, it wasn't going to be non-stop action all the way, was it? – and was ready to leave inside five minutes. My wife can make dawdling an art form, though, and, despite having had a hospital bag packed for the last week, it still took her an hour and a half to get ready. She insisted on first having a long bath and washing her hair, then getting dressed unbelievably slowly, and finally checking everything three times before pronouncing herself fit to give birth. It took all my self-restraint not to have a major row.

The car started first time. One panic over. Now concentrate, John. Don't take any chances. How am I

doing? Thirty-five m.p.h. Better slow down a bit. Watch out for the lights, they're about to go red. One last roundabout to go. Made it. I've got her to hospital safe and sound and in plenty of time. Well, that's my bit done. Over to you now, wifey.

The night porter let us in with a weary nod, and we made our way upstairs to the labour ward. We explained what had happened to a midwife who, having wired my wife up to a few gadgets, promptly disappeared and forgot about us. It was mildly disconcerting to be left alone, but for the most part I was in heaven. The winking electronics, the steady pulse of the heart monitor, the array of stainless steel surgical instruments, the smell of antiseptic, even the occasional shout and scream from a nearby room, were immensely reassuring. I was in the right place.

Two and a half hours later the midwife returned to give my wife a further examination.

'Nothing much is happening yet, dear.'

Please don't send us home, please don't send us home. Anything but that.

'I think you'd better go home and come back a bit later.'

This was a disaster. Instead of being able to lounge around offering a few tender words of encouragement, it was back to being Mr Responsible.

We got home at about five, and by then my wife was getting some noticeable contractions every quarter of an hour or so. This effectively prevented her from going back to bed, but I managed to doze off for a few hours.

After all, there was no point in both of us getting exhausted.

My wife was still wandering around the house when I woke up, and I resumed my vigil in front of the TV. For the next two hours it was desperately important that the contractions should not get any closer together. The fourth day's play of the third Test between Pakistan and England was about to start, David Gower was next man in, and he needed only a few more runs to overtake Boycott as England's leading run scorer. Go on, David, my son. You can do it. Four needed. *Yeah*. It had to be some sort of sign. Jo wasn't just going to be OK, she was going to be a genius, too.

Come the lunch break, my wife felt that the time had come to go back to the hospital. Having had a dummy run twelve hours earlier helped to stem the panic, and within forty minutes we were back on the labour ward.

'You're about six centimetres dilated, dear.'

Is that good news or bad news?

'So how long is it likely to be until the baby is born?'

My wife's contractions were now intense, and she wanted to work out her pain-relief options.

'It should be about another seven hours.'

'I can't last that long. Can you get me an epidural?'

'Sure.'

So I could take the bucket and the tennis balls back to the car for a start.

It took the anaesthetist a couple of goes to find the right spot, but, once in place, the epidural quickly did its stuff. Much to my own relief, the screaming stopped and my wife became almost mild-mannered and charming.

The next four or five hours were remarkably relaxing.

The sun poured through the window, making the labour room almost inviting, and my wife and I chatted about this and that and occasionally glanced at our books. The only person doing any work was Jo. To help her along I played a non-stop diet of Mozart, Schubert and Haydn on the tape machine I'd brought with me. This was the sort of music I'd have liked to have been born to, and I figured that if by any chance she didn't like it, she'd have plenty of opportunities to get her revenge later on.

At about eight thirty in the evening the midwife took a peek up my wife and declared that it was time to start pushing. This was the moment I had been dreading, because I still hadn't decided where I should stand. Was I going to loiter around the safe end, intermittently mopping my wife's brow, or was I going to get stuck in down the business end? The idea of getting first peek at Jo was immensely appealing, but cowardice was on the verge of winning out when the midwife said, 'I need you down here to help time the pushes.'

No choice then. I had to be a hero.

For once in my life excitement got the better of anxiety. Whether it was the thrill of being able to shout 'Push' at my wife and have her respond immediately, or the expectation of seeing Jo, I'm still not sure, but I began to enjoy myself.

'I'll just cut the cord to make sure it's not in the way, and then one more push and she's out.'

'Push.'

Hello, Jo.

Immediately I saw her I knew something was wrong. She was a translucent pale-grey in colour and completely inert. Keep calm, John. You know you're neurotic. You've never seen a newborn baby before. Maybe they're all like this.

A few seconds later the midwife pressed the crash bell, and a couple of doctors came tumbling into the room with a trolley. They placed Jo under what looked suspiciously like a grill, fed a tube down her nose, attached a drip to her hand and wheeled her away to intensive care. My wife was lucky enough to have slipped into post-birth shock and so she wasn't fully aware of what was going on, but I was struggling not to hyperventilate. 'She'll be all right,' I found myself saying, but I had no idea whether it was true. I just couldn't believe we could have come so far to have Jo die on us now.

'I'd better go along with Jo.'

My wife wasn't in great shape, but Jo was in worse, and I felt that she needed me more.

For the next forty minutes I sat watching the heart monitor as Jo lay in her incubator with a little perspex oxygen box over her head, learning how to breathe for herself. Once I trusted her to get through the next ten minutes without me, I nipped back to the labour ward to fetch my wife, and together we remained like limpets around her cot for over an hour until a doctor told us that he was confident she would be OK.

We never did find out what was wrong with Jo, and I still wonder what happened. Did my fear that she might die inspire her to give it a go? (Needless to say all the wives of the ante-natal class dads, who had never given death a thought, had trouble-free deliveries.) Or did my anxiety keep her alive, by ensuring she had some of the best staff and facilities in the country? Or maybe it was my choice of music. After two more days on the Intensive Care Unit, Jo was well enough to be transferred back to the maternity ward, and all that time she had listened to round-the-clock Capital Gold.

LIFE SENTENCE

'The midwife says I can go home on Friday or Saturday.'

'I think it had better be Saturday. Just to be on the safe side.'

I was trying to make it sound as though my only concern was that both Jo and my wife were strong enough to come home. But I was also worried about whether I was fit enough to have them home. Now that Jo was out of danger, I quite liked the idea of them both being in hospital. In fact, I wouldn't have minded had they stayed there for a couple of months or so. Maybe a year, even. It wasn't that I didn't want to be with them, I just wanted to know that they were both safe, and that I wouldn't have to worry about them the moment I left the room.

I'd also got into a nice little routine by myself at home. I would wake up, nip out to get the papers, and treat myself to a leisurely breakfast.  No noise, no interruptions. I would leave the house mid-morning, potter over to the hospital, hang around for the afternoon, and then come home and put my feet up for the evening. I could spend hours on the phone to various family members and friends, accepting their congratulations for Jo's arrival and commiserations for its manner, order a take-away, and relax in front of the TV. All fairly shallow stuff, I agree, but I didn't give a toss. Right then, it was the closest I could get to having a halfway decent feeling about being a dad.

After the initial relief and gratitude for Jo's recovery had passed, I was gripped by some altogether more difficult  and unpleasant emotions. Each morning when I saw Jo for the first time in hospital I would burst into tears. Now it wasn't the tears that were difficult, because I've been a bit of a cry-baby ever since I realized that a lot of women found it immensely attractive. It was the knowledge that came with them. I was frightened of letting myself go with Jo. I still wasn't 100 per cent sure that she wasn't going to drop dead any moment, and I was reluctant to get too close. And I felt dreadful about it. What kind of daddy tries to stop himself loving his three-day-old daughter?

I was also feeling extremely angry. I'd read my Penelope Leach and Sheila Kitzinger – I hadn't, actually, but I'd been bored so often by parents quoting them that it felt as though I had – and I knew that the first hour after birth was meant to be a special time when critical bonding took place. You were all three meant to cosy up on the bed in the labour room and get all lovey-dovey, and then give the baby its first feed. So what had happened to our magic hour? Why had I had to spend it like a headless chicken, while Jo lay all alone in her incubator getting her first feed via a plastic tube plugged into her hand?

Even if the birth had been utterly straightforward, I suspect that I would still have found the first few days somewhat trying. After twenty-four hours or so Jo had lost her scary vampire hue and turned a more healthy pink, but she still didn't look anything like what I had imagined. I wasn't entirely sure what I had expected – all I knew was that this wasn't it. Sure she had two arms, two legs and a head and she was obviously beautiful, but there was something not quite human about her. Perhaps she was a pet. What was equally frustrating was that she showed absolutely no sign of recognizing me. When she could be bothered to open her eyes, she would stare straight through me as if I was a stranger. So all those hours spent talking to my wife's tummy had been a complete waste of time.

Picking Jo up turned me into a nervous wreck. She was a normal weight for a baby, but I had never held anything so tiny, and I used to get all sweaty thinking about it. My body would stiffen and I would try to place my arms underneath her like a mechanical digger, to prevent her head from wobbling around too much. Once she was safely in place, all I could think about was dropping her. And sometimes it was bloody tempting, I can tell you.

After wandering around the hospital with her for a quarter of an hour or so, doing the regulation coochie-

coochie-coos and trying to get her to grab my finger in her fragile fist, I would then put her down and feel as

 blank as I had when I started. I had no idea what to do with a small baby, and I was just mindlessly repeating what I'd seen a few other dads do. Was she enjoying herself, or was she bored and irritated? Search me. No one has ever been able to make me feel inadequate quite like Jo.

All this time my wife was spending most of the day sitting on a rubber ring in bed. Jo hadn't made the tidiest of entrances and – to use the hospital parlance – my wife was suffering from a sore bottom. She was also looking completely knackered, as the incessant noise on the ward made sleep practically impossible. And I came over all protective of her. When she asked me to go on errands for her, I would find myself not only saying yes without a murmur but not even demanding any money up front. Relaxing your guard like that is not always to be recommended.

'I'd like a couple of sandwiches and a carton of orange juice from M & S, and some cotton wool and nappies from Mothercare.'

Note, I didn't even make her say please.

'Oh, I'll need some maternity knickers, too.'

Aaagh. Not maternity knickers. Not those horrid white net jobbies. I could just about cope with Tampax providing I got them from Sainsbury's where you could quickly chuck them in the trolley and pretend they're nothing to do with you at the checkout. But maternity

70

knickers were just too humiliating. And it goes without saying that they were hidden away in one corner of the shop so that I had to ask for them.

With my wife confined to bed, I got to control the telephone calls. This was an immensely powerful position and not one that my wife would normally have relinquished without a fight, but just then she was past caring and happy to let me get on with it. So it was totally up to me who got to hear first about Jo's arrival and who got the prime visiting slots. As such, it was an ideal time to settle a few old scores. Those of my wife's friends who had made even vaguely critical remarks about me – yeah, Karen, I bet you thought she wouldn't tell me – were immediately relegated to the back of the grid, while one or two of my own friends who frequently took more than twenty-four hours to return my calls got dumped next to last. I could be pretty busy, too, you know. With family, the main thing was to be extremely bossy.

'You can come at six thirty, but don't stay any longer than half an hour because we're all very tired.'

Perfect. I could sound completely at ease with my new role of responsible paterfamilias, and at the same time I could get my own back for years of being ordered around by my parents and two older sisters.

In between assignments and visits and stacking up the ever-growing mountain of cuddly toys, my wife and I would often just sit together with Jo and watch the world

71

go by. And I learnt that giving birth was a highly competitive business. Most mums came in and spent at least a night or two on the maternity ward. But there  were some who were unquestionably after their ante-natal class Duke of Edinburgh Gold Award; they would rush into hospital, give birth inside two hours – 'It was just so natural, darling' – and then dash home to knock up a little Sophie Grigson creation for dinner.

At the far end of the ward there was a woman who gave every sign of staying in as long as my wife. It didn't seem as though anything was wrong with her or the baby, but I was initially a little shy to ask. Just in case there was. On the fourth day, curiosity won out and I strolled over for a chat.

'Oh there's nothing wrong. I just went for an elective Caesarian so that I could spend a week in hospital. I've got three kids at home and I thought I'd get a damn sight more peace and quiet in here.'

Now, that was a woman after my own heart.

HOME SWEET HOME

The first two weeks at home are a time when you can enjoy getting to know your baby and begin to relax into a comfortable family routine.

In your dreams.

'Where's my lucky nipple shield?'

'I dunno.'

'Well, just find it.'

We'd been home from the hospital for barely fifteen minutes, and we were already in crisis. Within seconds of our arrival, Jo had started to shriek as loudly as she could. My first assumption had been that she was as freaked out as I was to be home, but as the yelling continued it dawned on us both that she was starving. For the child of an earth mother this would have been no problem. Tits out, lock on, and Bob's your uncle. Or not, in Jo's case. Her idea was to get attached and to chew vigorously until the nipples bled, and the only way my wife had managed to continue to breast-feed was with the aid of an industrial strength plastic nipple shield, which had been kindly donated by the hospital.

'I've looked everywhere. We must have left it behind.'

'Well, why didn't you check we had it before we left?'

Ah. My fault.

'I'll go back and get it, then.'

'That's no bloody use. Jo's not just going to shut up for the next hour. She needs feeding now.'

'So what do you want me to do?'

'Christ, I don't know. Make a bottle or something.'

'How do you do that?'

'Why don't you read the instructions and find out?'

OK, OK. I was only trying to save a bit of time. Now, where was I? Ah, yes. First, sterilize the bottle.

'Any idea how the sterilizer works?'

'For fuck's sake.'

'I take it that's a no.'

Throughout the fifteen minutes it took me to sterilize the bottle, boil the water for the milk and cool it to a drinkable temperature, Jo kept up a continuous wall of sound that veered between the plaintive and the angry, and occasionally went over the edge into outright desperation. When the bottle was finally ready, Jo peered at it with some suspicion for a few moments, before deciding to glug away. It clearly wasn't what she really wanted – no flesh and blood – but perhaps she realized it was the best she was likely to get under the circumstances.

Once Jo was tucking into her bottle, I nipped back to the hospital to get the lucky nipple shield. On my return, an air of comparative calm prevailed. This was as good a moment as any to introduce Jo to her new home. I

picked her up, walked her round the living room –
paying special attention to
the newly painted radiators
and skirting-boards – took
her upstairs to the bathroom
and bedrooms, and then
outside into the garden. By
which time she was fast
asleep.

Now it wasn't as though the tour had been terrifically
time-consuming or exhausting, it was just that sleep was
Jo's preferred state. When she wasn't having a temper
tantrum or feeding or crapping, she slept. This was very
disappointing. I hadn't expected Jo to be a bundle of
laughs from the off, but I had thought that she might do
a little more than this. I mean she was hardly a newborn
any more; she was five days old, for Christ's sake.

Jo's capacity for sleep was in inverse proportion to my
own. I had always found sleeping very demanding. I was
extremely good at getting to sleep and very bad at staying
that way. My eyes would close the second my head hit
the pillow, but I would miraculously find myself wide
awake within two hours, worrying about something I
hadn't even thought of before I had gone to bed. And Jo
made this much, much worse.

My dad had made Jo a beautiful wooden crib which
we placed by the side of our bed, and from the first time
she lay on the mattress she seemed to regard this crib as
her spiritual heartland. Mind you, she was extremely
tired that first night because my wife and I had kept her
up until eleven thirty. Neither of us really knew how to
put a baby to bed, and so we hadn't bothered. Instead, we

sat up watching the TV, taking turns to hold Jo. Now and then she would squawk for some milk, but for the most part she would lie restlessly in our arms, trying to get in a comfy position to kip.

Eventually we plucked up courage to put her to bed, where she stayed fast asleep for eight hours solid. I suppose that some parents would have been thrilled to have had a baby like this, but I found it hell. In my view, babies were supposed to wake up every few hours, and if they didn't then something was wrong. That night, I woke up at two o'clock, four o'clock, and six o'clock and each time, as soon as I realized that Jo wasn't making a peep, I had to leap out of bed to check she was still breathing. It wasn't what I needed, frankly, and I'm glad to say that Jo soon learned the error of her ways, and within days she had adopted a more conventional nocturnal time-table. This was much better. There's nothing like waking up to the sound of your baby gurgling and your wife yawning to let you know that all is well with the world.

So far, so banal, you might think. Slightly more hyper than most men's first few days at home with wife and baby, perhaps, but by no means the worst-case scenario. But then you, like me at the time, might have missed the sub-text to all this. Within minutes of starting family life at home I had become the world's supreme reactive being. Think about it. Baby cries – look for the nipple shield and boil some milk. Wife shouts – go to hospital to get nipple shield. Baby sleeps – I wake up to see if she's OK. Not one original or creative action throughout the whole day.

While my wife had been pregnant I had had anxieties

about a lifetime in service, and had been determined to guard against it. Well, as far as I could. And yet, there I was on day one slipping, willingly and unthinkingly, into the very role I most feared. I blame the milk, myself. The sight of Jo snuggling up to my wife's breasts was a depressing reminder of my status. It was my wife who could give Jo what she most needed, not me. So they had this cute little thing going between them, and I was pretty much surplus to requirements. And the more useless I felt, the more I tried to prove I wasn't by doing useful things – like fetching the nipple shield. Which only served to underline just how much of a second-class citizen I really was.

The trouble with acting like a slave is that you rapidly adopt a slave's mentality. I would try to maintain the illusion of freedom by investing my actions with more importance than they were due – so sterilizing a bottle became a one-man war against bacteria: 'You mess wid da princess, and I mess wid you' – but for the first time in my

adult life I found myself not questioning what was said to me. My wife would say that Jo needed this or that, and I would just nod and get on with it. Now some men might like to think that women are born knowing more about baby things, but then they're probably the sort of men who haven't realized they were born stupid. I was perfectly aware that my wife knew as little as I did about childcare, but instead of saying to her, 'How do you know?' I would metronomically defer to her ignorance.

My wretched mental state wasn't helped by my working

from home. Most men get only a few days' paternity leave from their jobs, which means that they can soon return to a nurturing environment where someone might occasionally say 'thank you' or make them a cup of coffee. Moreover, when they come home their wives are so grateful to see them that they forget to make their lives a misery. However, I had stupidly decided to award myself two weeks' holiday when Jo was born, which meant that I was at my wife and daughter's beck and call for the duration. Next time I won't be making the same mistake. I'm going to make sure I've got so much work on, I'll just have to disappear to my office. To write this book, for instance.

CHANGING TIMES

'Jo's done a poo. Will you change her?'

'Yeah. Sure.'

Except I wasn't, really.

Before Jo was born I had gaily wittered on about my willingness to change nappies, because I had noticed that this was the sort of thing mothers wanted to hear. Indeed there were some I knew who were completely fooled by it. Their partners would pay absolutely no attention to the child for twenty-three hours and fifty-five minutes of the day, but because they would waltz in for the other five minutes to change a nappy, they would be paid an endless string of compliments for being a 'committed, involved' dad.

Since Jo's arrival six days earlier I had somehow got away without having to put up. In hospital, Jo had tactfully decided that the best time to crap was when I wasn't there, and even when she first came home she had waited till I was engaged in some other lowly task. I suppose I was beginning to imagine that such happy

conjunctions might occur every day for the next three
years, when the call to arms went out.

My reluctance to get involved had nothing to do
with the practicalities. After all, the mechanics of
changing a nappy are quite literally a piece of piss. You
just persuade the baby to stay in one place for long
enough to peel off two tags – dead easy when they're
under six months – wipe the bum, smear on some cream,
manoeuvre another nappy into place and fasten it. We
weren't ecologically sensitive or hip enough to invest in
washable nappies, but even with them the extra demands
wouldn't challenge the average eight-year-old.

It wasn't laziness that spawned my aversion, though I

admit that may have played
a part. Who wouldn't rather
watch the footie? No, the
real reason was that nappy
changing involved sex and
pooing, and if any two

activities are closely linked in the male psyche with
shame and humiliation, then these are they. Which is
why men have always enjoyed them best in private. And
I was no exception.

My sexual fantasy world has always been a great deal
more imaginative, and, dare I say it, more active than my
real one. Don't do that in public, Kylie darling. Liz – how
are you, luvvy? Mwaah. Mwaah. Is half past ten OK?
Claudia B-A-B-Y. In my mind I could be some kind of
superstud, women would always be begging for it, and
what's more I would never have to bother with post-
coital conversation. OK, there's no need to have a go. I
never said it wasn't sad.

As for having a crap, I break into a cold sweat at the thought of having my morning read of the paper on the lavvy interrupted.

Changing nappies was a hands-on sexual experience and was therefore fraught with difficulties. I would try to avoid the issue by muttering 'baby maintenance', 'hygiene', 'caring' and 'essential' – probably in the same sentence even – but I couldn't get rid of it entirely. After all, having my dick inspected at the clap clinic was a sexual experience, albeit a thoroughly unpleasant one. No, changing a nappy was a hand-to-front-bottom, hand-to-back-bottom affair, and when it was my hands that were involved, words such as incest and child abuse came immediately to mind.

So how was I supposed to behave when I changed Jo's nappies? Was I meant to adopt a matter-of-fact, perfunctory style for bum wiping and cream smearing? And if I did, would Jo pick up on it and become phobic about pooing later in life? Or should I say to hell with it, and try to turn nappy changing into a fun experience? Should I let Jo luxuriate in the feel of the cream? At what stage did fun turn into something more sinister? Did paedophiles necessarily have any sense they were doing something wrong? There had to be a line somewhere between taking too little time and spending too long, but I was damned if I could ever be certain I had found it. And I was very worried that Esther Rantzen might be after me.

I have to say that the childcare books weren't much help here. There were endless tomes on such worthy subjects as breast-feeding and potty training but not one of them contained a section on 'How to be sure you're not abusing your children'. A startling omission; publishers, please note. I even thought about phoning a social worker for help, until I remembered that they were generally as clueless as me on the subject. So the doubts always remained, even if by the time Jo was out of nappies they were down to a malingering niggle. Still, I was much comforted by the fact that Jo was a girl. At least I didn't have to worry whether I was gay as well.

But perhaps I'm jumping the gun a little here. Before I could even think about the finer points of the affair, I had to discover whether I could survive close contact with a dirty nappy without gagging. And this was by no means a certainty, because I've never been big on coprophilia.

So it was with some surprise that I found that nappy changing could be almost pleasant. OK, there was the odd awkward moment when the nappy was so full that cack would escape out the top and I would have to make sure that my hands didn't get covered, but the main thing was the smell. For the first six months or so, Jo's poo gave off a faintly sweet, sickly smell which bore no relation to that emitted by the more familiar adult version, and there were times when I was changing her that I managed to forget about what I was doing.

Now this smell wasn't a mere figment of my imagination, drawn out of my unconscious need to turn something nasty into something nice – would that I were so powerful; it really existed. My wife claimed that it came from Jo being fed primarily on a diet of her gently perfumed breast milk, but that seemed far too self-serving and sensible to be true. I felt it was because Jo knew how difficult I would find it to deal with the real smell, and through some feat of gastro-intestinal alchemy, had provided me with something I could cope with. At any rate, that's what I wanted to believe, because it showed that Jo gave me the odd passing thought.

After a while Jo trusted me enough to know that I wouldn't leave her in a pile of cack regardless of the smell, and duly presented me with her first smelly turd. Maybe my senses had become so dulled over the previous six months that I would have cleared up almost anything, but I didn't find it as obnoxious as I had feared. There was the fascination of seeing the effect Jo's diet had on her digestion – I never could get over the way that sweetcorn would reappear looking exactly the same as when it was swallowed – but more than that, it was the excitement of watching her grow up. This was the first truly adult act that Jo ever performed, and I was immensely proud of her for it.

Not half as proud as Jo was, though, and by the time she was two years old and able to hold some kind of conversation, she wanted to subject each creation to prolonged analysis.

'Let me see it, Daddy.'

This would be her opening gambit, once I'd taken off the nappy and wiped her bum. My first inclination was always to say no and try to get on with putting on a clean nappy, but it was actually a reasonable request. She'd produced it and she had a right to look at it.

'OK. Just quickly.'

Five seconds later: 'I want another look.'

'No. One's enough.'

'Can I touch it then?'

'No.'

'Why not?'

'It's yucky.'

'Why is it yucky?'

'Look. If we get a bend on you can watch a bit of *The Jungle Book* on the video.'

Distraction is a great help in dealing with toddlers, but it didn't really work for me. Even though Jo had long since ceased to care about her last question, I was still struggling for a decent answer. How did you explain to a two-year-old child that something which had come out of her body was both perfectly natural yet at the same time unhygienic, without either confusing her or making her phobic?

With all these worries, you might have thought we would be keen to get Jo out of nappies as quickly as possible. But we weren't. For one thing Jo was in no hurry, and for another we had a shrewd idea that potty training would be even worse.

LEFT OUT

'Hi, darling. How's your day been?'

'Hell. Jo wouldn't feed properly and has hardly slept. I've been stuck indoors all day, and I haven't had a moment to myself.'

'Poor you. Well, I'm back to help out now.'

In normal everyday conversation this would have been the time for my wife to ask me how my day had gone. But we weren't living in civilized times. Jo was now a few months old and I was back at work. Generally this meant being shut in my office upstairs trying to get something written in between constant interruptions from my wife. She had always considered working from home to be a bit of a joke, and she saw absolutely nothing wrong with barging in whenever she felt like it to update me with some unnecessary information on Jo's miraculous progress. And without fail she would make it plain that it had little to do with me. That particular day, however, I had had to be out of the house all day.

'Well, my day went better than expected,' I offered.

'What?'

'Since you hadn't asked, I thought I'd let you know that everything had gone OK.'

'I could tell it had.'

Oh. So having a baby had turned her into Mystic Meg.

In truth, my wife was bored. She wasn't used to

loitering at home all day with no one to talk to. Jo still couldn't do very much, and my wife resented any sign of my having an independent existence.

Not that I felt very independent, mind. True, I had advanced a little from my abject servility of the first few weeks, but by no stretch of the imagination did I get equal billing. I was now allowed to make one or two arrangements of my own, but only if I had already fulfilled all my other duties. At first this rather went to my head, and I was forever inviting friends over for supper. But after a while the demands of shopping and cooking for extra people, not to mention the effort of talking to them, became too exhausting, and I soon reverted to a more isolated life-style. Still, it was nice to know that I could be sociable if I wanted to.

It was worth keeping up the pretence of sociability to fuel my wife's envy. The point was that she thought I was having a much better time than her, and it was vital not to disabuse her.

'Yeah, sorry I was a bit late. I bumped into Alex on the way home, and we stopped off for a drink together. He sends his love.'

I hadn't, of course, but I knew she wouldn't check. In actual fact I had been stuck in a traffic jam in Vauxhall for half an hour, and even my cabin-fevered wife wouldn't have considered that to be much of a thrill.

OK, so it was all a bit childish, but going out was the

only area where I had the upper hand and I wanted to make the most of it. You see, I was just as envious of her as she was of me. Because she had Jo. The more time I spent back at work, the more time my wife and Jo had together *à deux*. And I didn't need to be a genius to work out which parent I would love more if I was a three-month-old baby. Between the one who was there and the one who wasn't, it was no contest.

Which was one reason why I was surprised at the attitude of so many of the fathers I knew who boasted of how small a contribution they managed to get away with. 'I worked late two nights, and Helen gave me permission to go out with the boys on another, so I've only had to give the little one a bath once this week.' Oh whoopee. What a result. Some men just can't spot a hospital pass. Did they really believe that their partners had been overwhelmed by a fit of altruism or had slotted neatly into a safe sexual stereotype? Not a chance. Most women just aren't that dumb. They know that they're notching up points for the future. Come the teenage years it will be 'I love you, Mummy' and 'Up yours, Daddy'. And Daddy will have no one to blame but himself.

You might have thought that knowing all this would have given me a sense of perspective. It didn't. If anything it made it worse. I was so acutely aware of what might be going on behind my back that I became paranoid. While sitting at my desk I would imagine my wife worming her way

into Jo's good books. Even if she wasn't openly saying things like, 'Daddy isn't upstairs because he's working, you know; he's there because he doesn't want to

be with you,' I felt that she might well be thinking such thoughts and that they would be entering Jo's head through a process of

psychic osmosis. Well, I did say she had turned into Mystic Meg, didn't I? Strangely, it was often the lesser worries that preyed the most. I was older than most fathers and I could just see my wife whispering to Jo, 'Your dad's going to be forty when you go to school, and he's going to look a right loser in the fathers' race.' I tell you, I started getting fit there and then.

Talking about it didn't help, either, because my wife

didn't seem to understand my fears. In fact, I think she thought I was making them up. Only one woman I spoke to ever came

close to admitting that men got a raw deal, and that was completely by accident.

We had gone to a children's party, and I had found myself chatting to a hippy mother, who looked as if she had just spent three days at Glastonbury. I can't have been feeling too bad, because I started to talk about my sense of exclusion.

'Ah. You're suffering from the green-eyed monster.'

Now, that sort of primary-school teacherspeak normally makes me feel sick, but something struck a chord within me and made me hold back from outright sarcasm. It wasn't what she had said that was remarkable, because to all intents and purposes she was only repeating back to me what I had already told her. It was her tone. There was no surprise at all. Just total elation. Instinctively we both looked across the room at her partner – a derelict, emaciated by a force-fed vegan diet, with lank, scraggy hair and vacant, hollow eyes – and I knew she was counting the days till I reached the same level of physical and emotional destitution.

This encounter proved cathartic, because I vowed I would prove the hippy wrong. It was time to cut the victim crap, be a real daddy and tackle my wife head on.

THE WORM TURNS

The ending of maternity leave was my big break.

For all my wife's claustrophobia about the home, she was reluctant to go back to work. In part this was because she felt so guilty about abandoning Jo at six months, but mainly because she realized that her halcyon days as top dog were coming to an end.

She had delayed the inevitable for as long as possible,  by stretching out her maternity holiday for a couple of extra months, but the time came when she had to fix a definite date for her return. And it was a red-letter day in my diary – if not in hers.

Now I'm a great believer that babies aren't as stupid as they look, and that they're capable of dealing with much more information than most adults give them credit for. So I took it upon myself to let Jo know that her mum would shortly be around in the daytime only at weekends. Well, someone had to do it. Imagine how Jo would have felt if nobody had said a word, and one moment her mum was there the whole time and the next she wasn't. In any case, I like to think I handled it all very sensitively. I didn't tell Jo that the reason her mum was disappearing was because she didn't love her any more. I just pointed out that I would still be in the house – just as I always had been – and that I would be only a few yards from her at any time. And of course we would continue to have lunch together. Working from home was beginning to pay dividends.

Once my wife was safely back at work, the field was mine. It wasn't just that I could get on with my work without the threat of constant harassment, but also that I had a hold on my wife. Work was my wife's Achilles' heel, and she knew it. More importantly, so did I, and whenever she became too full of herself or I was feeling more depressed than usual I had a powerful form of redress.

'I don't think Jo recognized you when you got back this evening' was one of my earliest gambits, and I have to say it wasn't a great success. The aim was to sow a few seeds of doubt about her parenting skills, not to start a nuclear war. This attack was so ill-judged that my wife went  completely berserk with me for the rest of the evening. Which was self-defeating really, because it allowed her to take out her angst on me, rather than on herself as had been intended.

In time I became much more sophisticated in my

warfare. 'We've both been a bit wrapped up in our work lately, and I don't think that Jo's been getting the attention she needs' turned out to be much the best approach. It wasn't too over the top, and it implied some kind of mutual responsibility. But happily my wife would automatically assume that it must be all her fault because she believed that she was easily the more important parent.

Just where she got this idea from was another matter. Maybe it was the ringing endorsement of the £41.60 child benefit cheque that winged its way into her account each month, or maybe she was just copying every other woman she knew. Either way I wasn't happy about it.

The babycare books trawled a typically wishy-washy liberal line on the subject. They would go on and on about how parenting was a shared experience and how mothers and fathers should act as a team, but the implied message throughout would inevitably be that the mother was the skipper. And would you believe it? Some of these books were written by men. What a bunch of no-hopers.

No, the more I thought about it the more I realized my wife's case was far from proved. So, she could breast-feed. So what? I could give Jo a bottle. She could change a nappy. So could I. She could comfort Jo. Ditto. In fact, I could do some of these things better than her. I was a master of the nifty nappy change, and I was much quicker than her at getting Jo off to sleep. Something to do with patience, I believe. Indeed, after mature reflection it began to look as though there wasn't just room for doubt that my wife was the better parent, but that she was actually making a number of elementary parenting mistakes. It followed therefore that I was the better parent.

This revelation opened up some exciting possibilities, and the first thing I did was to take Jo into my confidence about it. And do you know what? I think she already knew. I would hold her tight and gently reassure her, 'It may not look like Mummy's being a good mummy at the moment, but I want you to know she loves you very much and she's doing the best she can. It's just that she's under a lot of  strain. Don't worry, though, darling, I'm here.' And Jo would glance at her mother with pity, and then give me a look which said, 'As long as I've got you, Daddy, I know everything will be all right.' At least that's what her look said to me.

With Jo securely on my side, it was time to let my wife know of my findings. Now, I would hate you to think that this was pure one-upmanship on my part. That was certainly a driving factor, but it wasn't the only reason. I had Jo to think of too, you know. I was very conscious of the need to limit the damage that could be done to her by my wife's worst errors. Understandably, this needed to be done with tact and delicacy, because no woman likes to be told how to be a mother. Especially if she doesn't know. Coming out with something direct like 'You're doing it wrong' would just have put her back up, whereas 'Have you tried doing it like this' was just the ticket. It sounded as though I was trying to be helpful but also carried the right measure of condescension.

It was the non-verbal communication that worked best, however. Although I had always tried to avoid it whenever possible, I had travelled enough times in the passenger seat while my wife was driving to become skilled in the art of the premeditated involuntary reaction. A wince here and a dash for an imaginary brake pedal there was guaranteed to make my wife frantic. And these tactics proved surprisingly adaptable. When my wife was playing with Jo I would wait until she was looking vaguely in my direction and then pretend to be absorbed in something else entirely while letting out a long-suffering sigh or drawing a sharp intake of breath. Invariably my wife would spin round and say, 'What's the matter?' To which I would reply, 'Oh. Nothing.' Deadly.

As Jo grew older, my wife's income became a bigger worry to me, because I was aware that there was a real risk she would try to compensate for her lack of natural parenting skills by buying her way into Jo's affections. She could have come home every evening with some new hideous toy, and I just wouldn't have been able to compete. Fortunately, Jo had no concept of money and was as likely to be impressed by a 20p piece of plastic as by anything substantial and expensive. Even so my wife did once bring home this extraordinary doll – made in Germany, need you ask – that you could tip water in one end and it would come out the other. Jo came perilously close to finding this interesting. I thought fast and asked her if she wanted a bag of crisps. She said yes and the danger passed. Incidentally, crisps, sweets and icecream never fail to repay their modest investment, as you can be assured of your child's undivided attention. You can't use them too often, though, because otherwise they get taken for granted. Oh yes – and they're bad for the teeth. I do have some scruples, you see.

For all the heavy competition to be best parent, Jo

showed herself to be annoyingly self-opinionated. On some days it would be me on whom she would lavish herself, and on others it would be my wife. And neither of us could ever detect a pattern to this. Which made it all the more important to make the most of the good days. Getting the winningest smile of the week was cause for a double celebration. It confirmed my pre-eminent status, and it really pissed my wife off.

Life meandered on in this up-and-down sort of way, but there were several moments that my wife and I both knew were  critical. As Jo slowly learnt to articulate sounds, we were both waiting for the moment when she said 'Mummy' and 'Daddy'. Logically speaking she had to utter one sound first, and whichever she chose would be very telling.

'Da Da.'

'Did you hear that?'

'No.'

Of course she had.

'Jo said Da Da.'

'She can't have. It's just some sort of phonetic accident. Besides, babies find it easier to say Ds than Ms.'

Sure. And O J was innocent.

About nine months later, when Jo was just beginning to talk in sentences, she came up to me and said words that she had never said to anyone before.

'I love you.'

Game, set and match.

HOME ALONE

'Well, go on then.'

My wife had been loitering around the front door for five minutes by now.

'Are you sure you'll be OK with Jo?'

'Look, you're only going out for the evening.'

'Celia's phone number's on the kitchen table.'

'You've already told me that.'

She had. Honestly.

'And you will ring me if anything happens?'

'Like what? An earthquake?'

'Promise me.'

'OK. Relax. Everything'll be fine. Now just go and enjoy yourself.'

Slam.

This was the moment that I'd been waiting for. My wife had thought that she was being monumentally trusting to leave me in charge for the first time, but I knew that going out was her unconscious's way of telling her that I was far better equipped to cope than she was.

Except that things changed the second my wife went out the door. It was easier to be a childcare expert when I had my wife on hand to criticize, but now that I was officially in control things looked a bit bleaker. Just what was I meant to be doing?

There we were. Just me and Jo. She was only a few months old at the time and not very chatty, so I picked her up, walked her round, sat down and switched on the TV. 'Do you mind watching the news? No? Oh good.' And after ten minutes of Carlton's *London Tonight*, Jo did what everyone else who is watching it does. Apart from switching channels, that is. She fell asleep. So far so good.

Fifteen minutes later things were suspiciously quiet. I leant over to check up on her breathing, and I thought I noticed that it was more uneven than usual. What if she was having respiratory failure? I thought about calling out the doctor. If Jo happened to be wide awake and screaming her head off by the time he arrived, I could always claim that she had made a miraculous recovery. And the real pay-off would be that he would be bound to give her a quick check-up so I could eliminate any other worries. In the end I decided against, because I thought he couldn't be trusted not to tell my wife at some time in the future. I didn't want to take any chances, though, and kept my ear closely pressed to her chest; when I still wasn't convinced of her well-being, I gave her a poke with my fingers. Whereupon she woke up.

'Whaaaaaa.'

'It's all right, darling. Daddy's here.'

'Whaaaaaa.'

'Do you want a bottle?'

'Whaaaaaa.'

'I'll just get it.'

'Whaaaaaa.'

Dash to the fridge. Hoik out the bottle. Bung it in the microwave.

'Whaaaaaa.'

Come on, come on. Ping. Phew. Fuck, it's too hot.

'Whaaaaaa.'

'Nearly ready.'

Rinse under cold tap. That'll do. Dash back to living room.

'Here we are.'

Glug, glug. Panic over. For now. What's the time? Christ, it's only seven thirty. There's at least another three and a half hours till Her Indoors gets back. OK, calm down. Deep breathing. That's better.

Half an hour later, and Jo was just about asleep again. It was time for the big one.

'Right, Jo darling, time for bed now.'

I was trying to sound confident – reassuringly paternal, so that even if she did wake up she wouldn't make a fuss. I'd put her to bed loads of times when my wife was at home, but this was a bit different.

Pick her up. Gently, now. G-e-n-t-l-y. Yes. Don't trip on the stairs. Into her bedroom. Put her in the cot. Wind up the musical mobile. Not a peep from the princess. I'm out of here.

I tiptoed back downstairs, and sprawled on the sofa  in a state of nervous exhaustion. Over the next hour I nipped upstairs a couple of times to check that all was in order – by which time I was feeling peckish. Such a magnificent display of fathering skills deserved a reward, and I picked up the phone to order a take-away.

'And you'll deliver it in about twenty minutes? Fine.'

A short while later the penny dropped.

You berk. You stupid great berk. It was too late to cancel the food and the doorbell would be bound to wake up Jo. So I spent the rest of my time hovering by the door waiting for the delivery man. Great. What an evening.

After supper, I started to tidy the house. Kitchen OK? Yeah. Bathroom OK? Yeah. Living room OK? Yeah. Check the watch. Forty-five minutes until the wife is due home. Time to settle down in front of the TV.

'Hi, there. I'm back.'

I didn't bother to reply at first. I wanted to make it look as though I had fallen asleep in front of the TV. This would have the advantage both of making me look incredibly nonchalant and of making her feel guilty for having got back so late.

'Hello-o. Where are you?'

She was sounding a little panicky now. Good.

'Uh. What?'

'Are you OK?'

'Yeah. I was fast asleep.'

'Is everything OK?'

'Sure. How was your evening?'

'Fine. Is Jo OK?'

'Of course.'

'What did you do?'

'We sat together down here for a while, and then I put her to bed and she went out like a light.'

'Did she cry much?'

Ah. She wants to know if Jo missed her.

'Not at all. She was terribly easy to be with. I can't

99

think why you make such a fuss when you're left on your own with her.'

That first evening was a salutary lesson in over-confidence, but all in all I was pretty pleased with the outcome. Jo had continued to breathe under my supervision, and I had managed to restore a sufficient sense of calm by the time my wife reappeared to unsettle her. Although Jo and I spent only about one whole evening a week together thereafter, we would get at least an hour alone every weekday evening in the period after I finished work and before my wife got back, and we quickly fell into a routine. When she was still very young this entailed nothing more than a bit of holding and maintenance, but as she grew more mobile and verbal we started to have a lot of fun, fooling about in the garden, reading stories, playing games or watching TV.

The problem with appearing competent was that it became inevitable my wife would one day start to take the piss. Sure enough, when Jo was about eighteen months old, my wife swanned in one evening to announce that later in the year she had to go to Zimbabwe and South Africa on business for two weeks. I was hard pushed to see how much work she was going to get done on safari in Victoria Falls but, call it work or call it freebie, I was going to be left holding the baby.

'Oh, that's nice. Don't worry about me and Jo. I'm sure we'll get by.'

'You could try and be a little more pleased for me.'

What?

'I'm sorry. No, it's great news, it really is. And I hope you have a lovely time.'

But it wasn't and I didn't. The trip was still six

months off when she first broke the news, so it wasn't hard to feign indifference, and apart from leaving the August rainfall statistics casually lying around, I barely mentioned her hols. As the date for her departure grew imminent, I found myself getting angrier and angrier, and I decided that reprisals were in order.

'Adrian phoned today and he's invited us to Scotland for a week. You can't come as you'll be away in South Africa but I said that Jo and I would love to go.'

Adrian's call had been a godsend. I knew that my wife was going to find it hard to leave Jo for so long, and the one thing certain to make her feel worse was the thought that we might be having a better time without her.

Now John's law of departures is always to make sure I'm the first to go, because it helps to stave off those unpleasant feelings of being left behind. So, bang on schedule, Jo and I hopped into the car eight hours before my wife was due at Heathrow, and we headed for Scotland.

The journey north was remarkably hassle free. Jo slept as far as Manchester and ate sandwiches and peered out the window until we stopped for a breather just south of Glasgow. She became a little more fractious as we  got closer to Fort William, but even so she was still in surprisingly good humour when we arrived. And so was I. The worst bit of the trip was over, and now I could get on with enjoying myself.

'Let's go out on the boat.'

'Don't want to.'

'I'll show you the seals.'

'Don't want to.'

'Why not?'

'Frightened.'

'I'll be with you. I'll hold you.'

'No. I'm frightened.'

And that was the pattern for the rest of the holiday. There was sod all for a two-year-old to do in that part of Scotland at the best of times, and Jo didn't even want to do that.

'Well, what do you want to do?'

'Be with you.'

I wanted to be with her, too, but I rather fancied doing some other things as well. But the only places where Jo felt really safe were inside the house or in the car. So that's where we spent most of our time. Now and then she would try to please me by consenting to go on a walk, but she always looked so bloody miserable that we abandoned it within twenty minutes.

'Telephone call for you, John.'

'Who is it?'

'Your wife.'

'Hello.'

'Hi, sweetie, how are you? I'm having a great time. A bit knackered, though. I was out till three last night at this amazing night-club in Harare.'

Just what I wanted to hear. My daughter was clinging to me like a limpet because her mum wasn't there, and her mum was getting blind drunk – or worse – in some sleazepit thousands of miles away. I was so depressed I couldn't even be bothered to give her a hard time.

The most difficult part of the week was the sheer relentlessness of it. If I wanted to go to the loo, Jo wanted to come with me. If I wanted to sit down, Jo wanted to sit on my lap. There would be a few hours' welcome respite after Jo had gone to bed, but these were mitigated by the knowledge that I stood a good chance of waking her when I  went up. Jo and I were sharing a bedroom, and her travel cot was wedged up tight against the bed. Too much noise and there would be a disaster, and there wasn't even enough light from the nightlight to read. It was just as bad in the morning. Jo seemed to have a sixth sense for knowing when I was awake, and within a nanosecond of me opening my eyes she would be on her feet, leaning over the edge of the cot, her bright blue eyes boring into my heart, shouting, 'Story.'

So we would have a story.

Holidays with friends were all very well, but not as a single parent, and I wasn't altogether unhappy to be off home at the end of the week. Jo clearly agreed and talked about nothing else for the first ten minutes. She then dozed off, and by lunchtime we were at the services outside Carlisle.

'Do you fancy a burger?'

'Yeah.'

'So do I.'

Error. Maximum error. It tasted great but I immediately needed a crap, and had to dash into a crowded Gents with Jo in tow, and squeeze us both into

103

a tiny cubicle. We'd just got back into the car when I felt another crap coming on. Jo couldn't quite understand  the urgency to repeat the procedure, but she gamely tagged along anyway. After that we at least got out of the carpark, but within five minutes of driving off I had uncontrollable diarrhoea. Every twenty miles or so I would have to pull off the motorway, regardless of whether there were services or not, and let nature take its course. I tried to turn the whole thing into a joke so that Jo wouldn't get worried, but I just wanted to die. Each time I stopped to squat by the side of the road, Jo would start waving her arms, screaming, 'Bye bye, Daddy's poo.' Bye bye, Daddy's life, more like.

To make matters worse Jo decided that this was the time to become a music fascist. Hitherto there had been some form of compromise between 'The wheels on the bus go round and round, round and round, round and round' and Radio 4, but now there was no negotiation. Every time I made a furtive attempt to switch to my station, Jo would shriek, 'My music, Daddy,' and keep it up until she got her way. Under normal circumstances I would have battled it out with her, but by then my spirit was broken. For the next five hours I meekly turned her tape over each time it finished, while I sat back and dreamt of London.

Life improved markedly once we got home. But the damage had been done and my wife had to be punished for it.

Jo and I got to Terminal 3 in plenty of time, and we picked a prime site by the railings in the arrival hall to wait for my wife to appear. Eventually the information board clicked up that her flight's baggage was in reclaim. It was time to give Jo her last briefing.

'Mummy will think it really funny if you rush straight past her and give a strange woman a big hug.'

That took the gloss off my wife's freebie, I can tell you. What's more she's never been away for more than two nights since.

THE HAND THAT ROCKS THE CRADLE

I've got a bit ahead of myself here. Before my wife could even think of going back to work, there were one or two practicalities that needed to be ironed out. Like who was going to look after Jo. We didn't live in Notting Hill Gate, which precluded the idea of a male nanny, but still left a vast array of women to choose from. My ideal would have been someone with access to full video-surveillance at all times, with her own armour-plated personnel carrier, and costing under £50 a week. Since we were unlikely to find this, we had to compromise somewhere.

'I think we should start by making a list of all the qualities we're looking for in a nanny,' said my wife.

'Good idea.'

'Being loving, gentle, imaginative, non-smoking, and able to drive are absolute musts.'

'And attractive.'

'What?'

'I'm serious. I think it's important.'

'So you can shag her, I suppose.'

'Don't be ridiculous.'

Even I wasn't that stupid. But I didn't see why I shouldn't be allowed to think about it from time to time. Since I worked from home I would probably have the most contact with the nanny, and it seemed absurd to pay for someone I couldn't stand the sight of. But obviously none of that was going to cut much ice with the wife, and so I had my little speech ready prepared.

'It's important for Jo.'

'How come?'

'It's common sense really. All the books say that an unattractive woman is more likely to have a negative self-image than one of average looks, and if we happen to choose someone who feels bad about herself she's bound to communicate that to Jo in some way. And however Jo turns out, we both want her to feel confident about the way she looks, don't we?'

'Hmmm.'

By the lack of an outright contradiction, I could tell that she was three-quarters convinced. It was time to go for the kill.

'I mean we're not talking sex kittens here. Just an ordinary, relatively attractive woman.'

Pause.

'OK. As long as she's only relatively attractive.'

So, despite some reservations about political correctness, relatively attractive got included on the list. Which was a great deal better than what I had feared my wife might insist upon.

For the most part, though, my wife and I displayed an

unusual consensus. We were both so driven with guilt at the thought of leaving Jo with someone else while we got on with our working lives, that we felt duty bound to spend as much as we could afford on the nanny. And what we could afford was for Jo to share a nanny with another family's child. We registered with an agency and set about interviewing possible candidates.

Nanny after nanny streamed through the front door.

 And they all seemed the same to me. They all had perfect references that identified them as latter-day saints, and they all had exactly the same replies to our questions.

'What would you do if Jo started crying?'

'I'd pick her up and try to find out what was wrong.'

'How would you keep Jo entertained?'

'I'd keep a nice balance between the fun and the educational. We'd go to the park, visit other children, read books – that kind of thing.'

'What would you give Jo for lunch?'

'I'd cook something fresh each day. No tinned or frozen foods.'

'What would you do if Jo consistently and wilfully disobeyed you?'

'I'd be firm without losing my temper. And if that didn't work I'd make her take time out on the bottom step of the stairs until she was ready to say sorry.'

It was almost impossible to tell who was sincere and who wasn't. Several of the nannies were extremely attractive, but even that had ceased to become an important consideration. I just wanted to find someone I liked. So the ritual had to go on. We knew it was a game, the nannies knew it was a game, but we had to ask the questions, and they had to give the standard answers.

Maybe it was because we were getting desperate – still no nanny and only a fortnight to go – but the moment Frances walked in, my wife and I both knew that she was the one who would get the privilege of looking after *la principessa*. She had a warmth and an energy that the Stepford nannies had lacked, and we all but hired her on the spot. We checked her references which confirmed her canonization, and met the other family for whom she was already working. They had the attraction of being even more chaotic than us, and we soon agreed terms. The deal was that Jo would spend one week at their home, and then Tina, the other child, would spend the next at ours. And so on.

And that was just about the last we ever heard of the deal. It worked OK for about a month, and then Jo began to spend more and more time at Tina's house, until she

had virtually taken up full-time residency. The problem, apparently, was me. In the nanny's view there was only one possible reason why I would want to work from
home – to molest either her or the children. It didn't matter that I was locked away in my office for long tracts of the day, venturing out now and again only to answer the phone or to make myself a cup of coffee. I was there, and it was bad. In the very early days I dared to join Jo and Tina for lunch, but Frances would always give me

such dirty looks that I quickly gave up on the idea. Instead I would cower in my office until I heard them leave the house, then dash downstairs to make a sandwich, and rush back upstairs as fast as possible in case they came back.

Before long I didn't have to cower in my office at all, because they were never there. I felt decidedly ripped off by this. We weren't getting what we paid for, and I was being robbed of seeing Jo. And I did precisely nothing about it. Yeah, go on, put the boot in, call me a wimp. I own up. I was. It had been hard enough to find Frances, and my wife and I couldn't face the idea of putting both Jo and ourselves through the trauma of getting another nanny, and we didn't want to say anything to Frances that she might take out later on Jo. Apart from anything else, Jo was blissfully happy with Frances. Even though I was never exactly sure what they got up to, I could see they had a ball. Now, I know that many parents like

 their children to be all washed and clean and in their pyjamas by the time they get home, but Frances never gave a toss about any of

that. And frankly neither did I. Jo would come home with a huge smile on her face, caked from head to foot in food, sand and dirt. And if it was OK with Jo, it was OK with me.

Ten months later, everything fell apart. I should have known something was wrong the moment Frances stayed longer than the usual five minutes in the morning to pick up Jo.

'Ruth's pregnant and they're planning to move out of the area.'

'Ah, well. I'm sure we can find another child to make up the share.'

'Um. I'm planning to go with them.'

'You're joking.'

'No.'

Brilliant. They get to change the arrangement unilaterally, and they get to keep the nanny.

So there was nothing for it. We would have to start again. Still, we weren't novices any more, and we had learnt some useful lessons. 1 – All's fair in love, war and nannies. 2 – Never, never, never be the junior partner in a share. My wife and I were agreed; there was no way we were going to get trashed second time round.

Angie seemed to be the answer to our prayers. She was a good deal more organized than Frances and she had already found another family with a little girl called Mary who wanted to begin the share on the same day as us. In due course we went to meet Mary's parents and we felt even more heartened. They gave the impression of being solid dependable types – no more unplanned pregnancies there. We didn't even mind when they insisted that the share took place in their house. At least I wouldn't be treated as a sex-offender.

At first all appeared to be going well. Or, to be more accurate, it didn't appear to be going badly because getting any information out of Angie about what Jo had been doing was like getting blood out of a stone. Angie held all men's parenting skills in open contempt, which made life extremely difficult as it was me who dropped off and collected Jo each day. I could be seen but not heard, and Angie certainly wasn't going to waste her breath by giving me the benefits of her childcare expertise. From time to time I would be brave enough to badger her for details, and she would raise her eyes long-sufferingly before deigning to reply.

'So what have you all been up to today?'

'What do you mean?'

I told you she didn't make it easy.

'What have you been doing?'

'I see. Gym in the morning, lunch, Hester's in the afternoon.'

I wasn't really any the wiser, but I didn't want to push my luck. I tried another tack.

'And how was Jo?'

'Fine. Why shouldn't she be?'

No joy there either.

'Any problems?'

'Yes. Jo didn't sit on the floor to drink her juice.'

Angie always brought our conversations to a close by mentioning something absurd like this. She wasn't noted for her sense of humour, but I assumed that this was her attempt at a joke, so I would chuckle along politely and say nothing.

Every evening when my wife got home, she would start to grill me about Jo's day, and would get immensely frustrated when the best I could come up with was, 'Gym in the morning, lunch, Hester's in the afternoon.' I think she thought that I was deliberately withholding information from her. Would that I had had the information to withhold. Still, I wasn't a complete bastard and I did reassure her that there were no problems.

After about six months of this, Angie summoned us.

'You're not taking me seriously.'

'Yes, we do. We think you're doing a great job.'

'Well, why does John constantly undermine what I'm doing?'

'I don't.'

'Yes, you do. I tell you something like Jo wouldn't drink her juice on the floor, and you just laugh at me.'

'This is the first I've heard of any of this. Why didn't you tell me about it?'

I was waiting for my wife to start kicking me when I was down.

'I didn't think it was important. I thought Angie was joking.'

'Well, it isn't important, but I want to know about it anyway.'

My wife had just dug her own grave.

'It is important. I happen to take my job extremely seriously, and I think these things matter. I shall expect more support from you in future.'

At that point, my wife and I were suitably penitent, and promised to be more encouraging towards her. Thereafter it was downhill all the way.

Jo probably couldn't have cared less whether she drank her juice sitting on the floor or standing up, but now I knew Angie was serious about it, I became convinced that she was trying to turn Jo into some prissy little yuppy. It got so bad that I couldn't think of Angie  without imagining her in uniform. And it wasn't even especially erotic. Getting proof for my suspicions was extremely tough. Jo seemed OK when I picked her up, but was this because she had been brainwashed by the Boot Camp regime? Was her refusal to say goodbye to Angie the normal action of a stroppy, tired two-year-old or a healthy reaction to being treated like a prisoner-of-war all day? Sometimes I would spy on her by peering through the letter-box for five minutes prior to knocking on the door in the evening, but Angie was far too clever to be caught out that way.

Angie continued to treat me with disdain, and so getting any real information about what was happening was next to impossible. After a few months, when the tension became unbearable, my wife and I decided we had to say something to Angie about it. As ever, we couldn't agree who should say it.

'I think you should talk to her about it.'

'No, you should.'

'No, you.'

'You do it. You're the one who sees her every day.'

'But she thinks men are useless. She'll listen to you.'

Amazing. A company director and a hack too frightened to tell their nanny where to get off. It was enough to make Jo weep.

Luckily we were soon put out of our misery by another summons from Angie.

'Sarah's pregnant.'

'Ah.'

'So I don't want to cope with three children.'

'Ah.'

'And it wasn't really working out between us.'

'No.'

114

That was assertive, wasn't it?

'So I think you'd better find another nanny.'

'OK.'

So that was it. Angie had given us the sack. And it was undoubtedly one of the biggest favours she ever did us.

After Angie, we felt so guilty about what we had put Jo through that we were prepared to risk bankruptcy by having a nanny to ourselves. That way we'd be able to keep a closer eye on what was going on, and if anyone got pregnant we would have only ourselves to blame. And we weren't going to take any more crap from nannies who found it difficult to work when their employers were around.

Third time lucky. We still asked the same pointless questions at interviews, and still got the same pat answers, but Catherine was a little different from all the others. Not only did she get lost on the way to our house and turn up half an hour late, she also laughed at my jokes. More importantly she laughed at Jo's jokes, and she got the job. And on the second day that Catherine worked for us Jo did something she had never done in all the time she was with Angie. She spontaneously flung her arms wide open to give Catherine a hug and a kiss.

Who says that money can't buy you out of trouble?

HELP

I've got a confession to make. You remember all that stuff I said about being the better parent a few chapters back? Well, it wasn't always like that. For all the joyous moments of rampant megalomania and point scoring over my wife, there were periods of prolonged depression. What if I wasn't just a worse parent than my wife, but a terrible father full stop?

There was some consolation in knowing that I couldn't be the worst father who had ever lived, but not much. Just because I couldn't be ranked on a par with child-killers didn't necessarily mean that I could be placed that much higher. Hadn't I thought about dropping Jo when she was first born, and who can tell how close a thought gets to action?

The problem was that I really didn't have a clue about what being a good dad meant. My own father had been rather a distant figure to me when I was young. His job regularly took him away from home and even when he was around he gave the impression of being a somewhat furtive character, anxious not to intrude on the family that my mother had created in his absence. We became much more intimate as I grew older, and he frequently told me how much he regretted not being closer to me in the early days. Which was good to hear, but not much help to me as a role model. Being a father was something that I had to make up as I went along.

My early efforts at being a dad involved being a mum. Or what I imagined being a mum to be. I would watch whatever my wife did very carefully, and try to duplicate it – only better. If she held Jo for half an hour, I would make sure I did it for thirty-five minutes. And so on. Now there was bound to be some overlap with my wife and it was comforting to feel close to Jo, but deep down I wanted my own sphere of operations. And though I don't suppose that any of this did her any harm, what Jo really wanted was a mummy and a daddy – not two mummies.

Maybe I was doing exactly what Jo wanted of me, but I would often look into her eyes and imagine she had expectations of me that I just wasn't meeting. Whenever she got angry – the milk was too late or she was facing in the wrong direction – she would put on this exasperated expression which seemed to say, 'It's just my luck to get a real cretin for a dad.' Even when she appeared to be perfectly content, I would wonder if I was failing her. Was the only reason she was smiling a desperate attempt to stop me looking so bloody miserable?

So how was I to make the transition from Mummy to Daddy? What would mark me out to Jo as being different to Mummy? For most men I knew the answer seemed to lie in making a lot of noise and doing bugger all, but I couldn't bear the idea of forever being identified as the sub-species whom Jo only ever turned to when Mummy wasn't there. I didn't just want to be different to a mummy, but special with it.

I thought that not shaving might help, because Jo would be able to run her hands across my face and feel the difference between myself and my wife. But Jo hated the feel of my stubble and cried every time she touched it. Besides which the only physical difference that Jo

was really concerned about at that stage was my breasts – or lack of them. Second best again. I tried not using any deodorant to let Jo get to know the Daddy smell, but my wife soon put a stop to that on aesthetic grounds. No matter what I did I seemed to get rejected. If it wasn't already hard enough being a man, then being a daddy seemed nearly impossible.

'I'm going to put the baby bouncer up.'

'You're joking.'

'No.'

'But you're useless at DIY.'

It was true. I was virtually useless at DIY. I could just about handle a paintbrush, but anything more technical involving drills and saws was completely beyond me. But

I was determined to give it a go. I was OK on the touchy-feely bits of daddying; it was the more manly, practical stuff that let me down.

As I saw it, daddies did things, and it was time I started doing things. OK, this was all very sexist, but who was to say that Jo didn't expect it of me? Maybe she had her own preconceived gender stereotypes and couldn't understand why I hadn't been off out the whole time killing things for the family pot. In any case if I didn't put up the baby bouncer, who would? Certainly not my wife, I can promise you. Go on, ask her.

The baby bouncer had seemed a great introduction to DIY – not too difficult, but not too easy either. Most baby bouncers fit simply on either side of a door, but we had no suitable doors, and I needed to attach two wooden struts to a beam in the ceiling to make ours work.

And I made a complete balls-up of it. My wife had a good sneer, but for once I didn't care because Jo was as impressed as hell. I authoritatively drilled a few holes here and there, and once I realized that I didn't know what to do next, I told Jo it was bathtime. I then put her to bed, and asked a friend over to finish the job. The bouncer was up and bouncing by the time Jo got up the next morning, and as far as she was concerned it was all down to me.

Buoyed with this success, I took it upon myself to introduce Jo to a range of experiences which my wife was bound to ignore. Before she could walk, this involved sitting her in front of the video to give her lessons in the history of English cricket and football and, as she became mobile, I included handy gardening hints and trips to McDonald's. I've got to say that while she remained a little hazy on David Gower's batting average and the different types of clematis, she was thrilled to bits with McDonald's.

I can't take all the credit for working out an MO as a dad. Jo deserves praise, too. Once she was old enough to talk, she made it abundantly clear what she wanted to do with whom. Some activities were both-parent jobs, some were just-Mummy jobs, and some were just-Daddy jobs. Mind you, nothing was set. One day pushing the buggy was a Mummy job, and the next it was a Daddy job, and when it was my turn I was happy to do it. While most major new events, such as first day at nursery school, were deemed two-parent jobs, there were some that were not. For some reason, going to the dentist was a just-Daddy job. And so off we went.

Even so, I never managed to eradicate all my fears of being a useless dad. I worried that Jo might think there was something wrong with me for going upstairs to work when every other dad she knew went out. I worried that there were things that I was doing that I shouldn't be doing, and that there were things that I should be doing that I wasn't. I worried. Let's leave it at that. I suppose I could have asked Jo whether I was doing all right, but it didn't really seem to be fair on her. Besides – she might have told me.

LOVE AND WAR

'I couldn't bear it if something awful happened to Jo.'

'Neither could I. It would just be the worst thing imaginable.'

Every few months or so my wife and I would begin conversations along these lines, but they would invariably peter out almost immediately. For a start, thinking about what could go wrong tended to bring me out in panic attacks, and, for another, they were a disagreeable reminder of how much our relationship had changed.

Before Jo was born my wife had been unquestionably number one in my affections, and I in hers. Since Jo's arrival, things had altered. It wasn't that my wife and I loved each other any less – if anything we might have loved each other a little more. It was just that Jo had a unique hold over both of us. If anything happened to me, I was confident – ish – that my wife would be very sorry, but I knew that she'd get over it and manage. If anything happened to Jo, I was pretty certain that she wouldn't. And I felt exactly the same way.

Knowing that my wife would race straight past me in an emergency, giving only the most cursory backward glance, en route to saving Jo was not the securest of feelings. And once I knew the score, I immediately ran out and bought a whole stack of smoke alarms. Not just for Jo, but for me. I didn't fancy being caught at my blazing bedroom window while my wife and daughter were standing on the lawn, yelling, 'Jump.'

The first people I ever loved were my mum and dad. I'm not exactly sure when I knew I loved them, but I think it was when I realized that I minded when they weren't there. So obviously I was in for a great deal of trouble, as parents have a habit of making you do a lot of dodgy things. Like going to school. Now there are various grades of schools that parents can send you to, and mine chose to send me to the worst – a boarding school. Which I took to be a punishment for not loving them enough, and a place where I should learn to love them more. After a week's incarceration, I wrote to my parents telling them that I had come to my senses, that I would try to be a better son, and would they please come and take me away. Perhaps the letter got censored by the school police, or perhaps my parents ignored it; either way, nothing happened, and I realized I was interned for the duration. So I discovered that love was a dangerous emotion, and that the best way to get by was to pretend that other people didn't matter much.

And that's how things stayed until my mid-teens when I discovered girls. My early encounters were fleeting, alcohol-inspired affairs – or rather, gropes – at parties. Now I know that these were largely exercises in lust and experimentation, but call me romantic, or call me confused, I used to think there was some love involved, too. If the girl let me French kiss her she loved me a little, if she let me touch her breasts she loved me quite a lot, and if she let me touch her down there then she loved me a great deal. It was a crude measure of intimacy, but it was the only one I had. By choosing to spend the evening with me rather than any of the other spotty adolescents hanging around the dance-floor, and by allowing me to interfere with her – and sometimes even interfering with me – the girl was showing me that I was special and that she wanted me. And that's what I called love.

Of course, I never told any of these girls I loved them. I was well enough versed in hip and cool to know that you had to have been going out with a girl for at least a couple of weeks before you said that. And since most of my affairs had lasted less than an evening, it was out of the question. Even though I often felt like it.

There came a time after I had left school when I had the opportunity to go out with the same girl every day for a fortnight, and, bang on cue at the end of that period, I told her I loved her. After a couple of moments to mull it over, she said she loved me too. And from that moment I think I really did love her in a teenage sort of way.

That relationship continued until she shagged someone else. And that was the pattern for quite a while thereafter, until I met my wife.

I thought I had love cracked with my wife. For the first time I felt safe with someone. Sure, I loved her for her looks and her intelligence, but just as importantly I loved her because she wanted to be with me and had stayed with me. And I wanted to stay with her, too. Over the years, she had learned to laugh at my jokes and to accommodate my neuroses – well, most of the time – and we had shared our hopes and dreams, and gone a long way to making some of them come true. We had become a team.

Then along came Jo, and it was like having an adrenalin shot to the heart. Jo made me feel in ways I just hadn't believed possible. All my life I had craved someone who would need me and love me unconditionally; now I had just that, I wasn't sure I wanted it. I knew that to love Jo properly would mean giving her the freedom to leave me at some point in the future, and I found it unbearably sad.

Still, there was a long way to go before running off with the milkman became a serious worry, and my most immediate concern was how to be a loving dad. It was all very well having the theory, but what did you do? Not for the first time, it was Jo who pointed me in the right direction.

For the first six months of her life Jo was rather dull. Cute and lovable, but definitely dull. She'd lie around for days on end, and the only way you could tell if you were doing anything right was by the absence of crying, and the odd, random smile. But the moment she learnt to sit up she became much better company. Jo and I

 would sit together on the floor; I would try to impress her by balancing her toy building blocks on top of each other, and she would knock them down with an aggressive backhand swipe. She thought this was hilarious, but I found it annoying because I was never given the opportunity to see if I could manage all twelve.

Big deal, you might think. All kids her age do that. Yeah, but it was the effect it had on me that was significant. Up till that moment I'd never been able to

have two feelings at the same time. If someone I loved pissed me off, then my love for them got temporarily suspended until my anger had died down. At least that was how it felt. But with Jo it was different. She could irritate me like mad, and I would still find her utterly adorable.

Now I dare say there are some people who can do this sort of thing effortlessly, but for me it was a revelation. It was something that I had heard about, but dismissed as a ridiculously Utopian idea out of some American book of happy-hippy self-improvement psychobabble. It was also something that applied only to Jo. I would have liked to extend my largesse to my wife – if only in the hope that she might return the favour – but it wasn't something over which I had any control. It was clearly the daddy love I had been looking for.

Once Jo cottoned on to what was happening, she was quick to take advantage. Offences, such as switching off the TV when the footie  was on, which would earn my wife lashings of tongue pie, would earn Jo only a gentle, patient telling off. So she did it again. And again. And again. Great. You try to act like a grown-up and all that happens is your daughter doesn't take you seriously.

It was losing my temper that made the difference. Now, it would make me feel a lot better to say that I lost it over something life-threateningly serious, like running out into the road. But I didn't. I lost it because she dropped her sweet wrapper. Jo had been winding me up ever since we got in the car. Three times she had dropped the damned thing, and each time she had yelled, 'Get it, Daddy.' Each time I had leant over to pick it up, but on the third occasion I had added, 'That's the last time.' Within ten seconds the wrapper was back on the floor.

'Get it, Daddy.'

'No. I said I wouldn't pick it up again.'

'GET IT, DADDY.'

'No. You'll have to wait till we stop.'

'GET IT, DADDY.'

'No. I've said no and I mean no.'

'WHAAAAA. WHAAAAA.'

The howling continued for a couple of minutes.

'Look. For God's sake bloody well shut up. I've had just about enough of you today.'

The howling stopped. Shortly afterwards we had a cuddle and made up, yet I still felt lousy that the only way I had been able to exert my authority over my daughter was to frighten her.

The short-term effects were wondrous, the long-term less so. Jo now knew my breaking point, and she would specialize in pushing me to within a whisker of losing my temper, only to come over all compliant and obedient just in time. Moreover she never liked to give me the satisfaction of thinking that she had in any sense deferred to me. After one particularly tense half-hour battle over getting dressed, I dared to say to her, 'That wasn't so bad, was it?' To which she replied, 'I was too tired to care.'

Well, how else would you have expected her to behave? Just look at her mum.

DOCTOR DOCTOR

'She's your first child, isn't she?'

Wow. Not just a doctor but Sherlock Holmes, too. Let me see. What could have given it away? Could it have been the absence of any other children running around the house? Could it have been there were no toys lying around?

'How do you know?' It doesn't pay to get sarky with doctors. They might kill you.

'She's only got a cough. There's nothing to worry about.'

'I see. Well, thanks for coming anyway.'

'No problem.'

And he actually sounded as though he meant it.

 Which is more than I would have managed if I'd been dragged away from home for no good reason on an August Bank Holiday Sunday.

But it had seemed like an emergency at six thirty in the morning. After all the dramas of Jo's birth, I had become attuned to the slightest variations in her breathing pattern, and when I was awoken by the sound of something like a death rattle coming from her chest, my heart went arhythmic. My wife needed to be awake.

'There's something wrong.'

'What time is it?'

What the hell did that have to do with anything?

'Something's up with Jo. Listen to her.'

'What did you have to wake me up for? She's just got a cold.'

'Well, I'm not happy. I'm going to call the doctor.'

'Hold on a mo.'

My wife got out of bed to give Jo the quick once-over. For all the noises bubbling from within her, Jo didn't seem to be in any distress. She had no sign of a temperature and was snoozing peacefully, and my wife prevailed on me to hold back from doing anything drastic. For the time being.

'OK, then. But if she's no better after breakfast, I'm going to get him out.'

'If you must.'

This was an unusually quick capitulation. For all her apparent sang-froid it looked as though she was secretly as worried as me. It was time to find out.

'No. You're right. It's probably just a cold. We'll see how she is tomorrow.'

'No, no. You go ahead and call the doctor if it makes you feel better.'

'No. I don't think I'll bother. You've made me feel OK about it.'

Pause.

'Maybe we'd better, you know. Just as a precaution.'

Gotcha.

So the poor unfortunate doctor was made to come

out. And if we ruined his day, he sure as hell made ours. Going to sleep knowing that there was nothing seriously wrong with Jo was the sort of reassurance that therapy just can't buy.

Two weeks later I was worried that Jo might be deaf. I'd vaguely remembered this experiment from my time at college, where some shrink had made clicking noises in a newborn baby's ears and had proved, by the movement of its eyes, that it could hear. Jo had two months' start on the control baby, and yet when I tried this out on her, she either looked completely blank or gawped in the opposite direction.

So I bullied the health visitor into booking Jo in for a full hearing test at the hospital. I can't recommend this too highly to other parents. The doctor stuck sensors to

various parts of Jo's body and then wired her up to some earphones, while she lapped up the attention and gurgled happily. After ten minutes of staring at several VDUs, followed by the examination of a computer print-out, Jo was deemed to have perfect hearing. Even better, we had something down in black and white to prove it. And very useful it's been, too. Whenever Jo conveniently claims not to be able to hear me, I've got something to show her.

On the way out of the hospital, I was struck by a thought. If there was nothing wrong with Jo's hearing, maybe there was something wrong with her eyesight. I'm proud to say that I kept this worry to myself and let nature take its course, and, touch wood, Jo has had no major health crises since.

I wish I could say the same for myself. As Jo has gone from strength to strength, I have lurched from one life-threatening illness to another. Or at least that's the way it has felt at the time.

Getting ill never bothered me much before Jo. Until I gave up smoking I would get an annual bout of bronchitis or pneumonia, which seemed no more than fair dos for the other fifty weeks of self-punishment. After I quit, I would get the odd snuffle or, at worst, a minor dose of flu, and that was just about that.

Since I first thought about becoming a dad I've had a suspected case of Aids, suspected bowel cancer, a suspected heart attack, and two suspected brain tumours. On each occasion the suspicion, I might add, has been entirely mine. Jo has turned me into a hypochondriac.

Whenever I got a symptom that lasted for more than twenty-four hours, I thought I was going to pop my clogs. Well, that's the way it used to be. Now I find myself worrying immediately a symptom appears because I know that if it hasn't gone within a day, then I'm in deep trouble. As soon as the first period of worrying time is up, I dive for the medical dictionary and allocate myself the first compatible serious condition. Let me explain.

A week after the diarrhoea attack nailed me at the motorway services on the way back from Scotland, I still had an upset stomach. Listed among the many possible inconsequential reasons for this in the dictionary was bowel cancer. So that's what I had, and I was under a death sentence. I voiced my fears to the doctor. He poked and prodded in a few embarrassing places, before declaring me cancer-free.

'Are you sure?'

'Yes. I think I can say I'm pretty confident about it.'

'But not 100 per cent certain?'

'Almost, but not definite. Only a barium enema would rule it out completely.'

Which is how I found myself in hospital a few days  later undergoing the indignities of a barium enema. Having a tube shoved up my bum wasn't much fun, but the feel of the gunge sloshing around inside me was somehow comforting. As were the parting words of the doctor.

'You're absolutely in the clear.'

I felt so good, it never even occurred to me to double-check that time. And do you know what? My diarrhoea cleared up within a day. Who can doubt the curative powers of modern medicine?

My other terminal complaints took on similar life-cycles. Within days of an old friend dropping down dead with a heart attack – see, these things do happen to people like you and me – I started to get some nasty twinges in my upper thorax and stabbing pains down my left arm. It took a stethoscope, a blood pressure check, an ECG, and a cholesterol test to sort that one out. My first brain tumour turned out to be a sebaceous cyst and my second a migraine.

I hope you're finding all this amusing, because I'm not. Well, not very. I can see it has its funny side, but it's no joke when I'm going through it. I know that I'm being neurotic and that there's almost definitely nothing wrong with me, but I just can't help myself. It's the 'almost' that gets me every time. You see, being alive has never been more important to me than it is now, because I want to be around to see how Jo grows up. And wanting something this much makes me very nervous, because it would be the ultimate sick joke to have emerged unscathed after taking the piss out of my body for years on end, only to be struck down by some fell disease once I had become the clean-living man about home. And I've always been very partial to sick jokes.

To complicate matters further, no one – except me – takes my health seriously any more.

'I've got a funny pain at the top of my neck.'

'It's probably another brain tumour.'

Howls of laughter from the wife.

'Do you really think it might be?'

'Oh, for God's sake. It's just a pulled muscle.'

OK. It was a pulled muscle, but that's beside the point really. One day – it might be tomorrow, or it might be in forty years' time – I probably will get a critical condition. And if I were to give in to my wife's line of thinking, I would probably be beyond help before I ever got to a doctor. My way, if I do get cancer, then at least it should be caught in the early stages.

See you in heaven.

SIMPLY THE BEST

'Jo's looking particularly gorgeous today, don't you think?'

'Yeah, but then she always does.'

If there was one thing that my wife and I could be relied upon not to argue about, it was this. By a remarkable genetic coincidence we happened to have the most beautiful, intelligent and physically able baby girl imaginable, and we felt obliged to remark on it at least once a day. Not to put too fine a point on it, we felt very lucky. We just couldn't picture how we would have coped if we had ended up with one of those ugly, clumsy retards that all our friends and acquaintances seemed to have been lumbered with.

It was a little more difficult to agree on who had given Jo what.

Jo was almost a dead ringer for my wife, and only the colour of her eyes – a matchless blue, since you ask – gave any indication that I had had anything to do with her conception. And from this my wife inferred that there was a similar genetic apportionment to Jo's internal configuration.

'She's got my brains, you know.'

My wife isn't thick, but even so this was insulting. Both to me and to Jo.

'I think you're underestimating her a bit. I suspect she's more like me in that department.'

'Don't be so bloody arrogant.'

'I'm not. I'm just stating the truth. I'm cleverer than you.'

'Why? Just because you've got more qualifications than me?'

'Well, that'll do for a start.'

'All that proves is that you're more of an anorak than me. In any case, if you're so clever how come I earn more than you?'

Now that is something that Jo has got from my wife. They both love to have the last word.

Jo's innate superiority caused problems from time to time. There's an etiquette among new parents that demands that everyone is fantastically complimentary about each other's sprogs. I used to dread these conversations. People would take one look at Jo and remark on her good looks and I could tell that they genuinely meant it. I knew that this was the cue for me to deliver a eulogy to their progeny, but what could I say about something so blatantly sub-standard? At first I tried to do the right thing by saying, 'Yours, too,' but I could never hide the insincerity in my voice. I then tried accepting the compliment in the spirit in which it had so clearly been offered and would just say thank you, but this didn't go down too well either. Finally, I compiled a dictionary of suitable return compliments. If the baby was fat I would say, 'He feeds well, doesn't he?' and if she was ugly I would say, 'She's growing into her features now, isn't she?'

There were, I'm afraid, one or two people who were

so eaten up with envy and competitiveness that they couldn't bring themselves openly to acknowledge how wonderful Jo was. I can't remember exactly who they were, though, because their names were instantly scrubbed out of my address book, and I've never bothered to make contact with them since.

Things get a little trickier now. You see, when my wife and I were warbling on about Jo's charms, we were really talking about our own. Having a child gives you the perfect excuse for boasting about yourself under the guise of praising someone else. If Jo was good-looking, where else did she get it from but us? If she was intelligent, ditto.

OK, OK. Hold on. Before any of you sanctimonious old bores start going on about how we're all unique, I'd just like to say that I agree with you. Up to a point. But look at it this way. Would you expect any member of the Royal Family to be bright? Like it or not – and believe you me, I do – children are a reflection of the parents.

I wasn't always so thrilled about this. When I was at school all my friends knew exactly who my parents were without being introduced, because only people who turned up in a tasteless old Austin Maxi could dream of dressing their son in a pink nylon shirt with light blue tie, offset by a dun-coloured corduroy jacket. It took me years to get over that.

Of course, with me for a dad, Jo would have no such style worries, and with a clear conscience I set about the process of trying to turn her into a civilized human being. It's all very well being gorgeous and intelligent, but, as we all know, it's what you do with it that really counts.

Now, the childcare books all tell you that children develop at different rates, and that just because one child starts walking later than another it doesn't mean that there's anything wrong. Well, they would say that, wouldn't they? Otherwise no one would buy the books. You just ask any parent what they really think. Of course it matters. Slow children, slow parents – we all know that. Which is why I was to be found on my hands and knees trying to get Jo to crawl when she was three months old.

Parents have a terrible habit of lying about their children's capabilities.

'Grace has started to feed herself already.'

My wife had been out for a walk in the park, and had bumped into another mum she knew. And what she was reporting back was seriously bad news, as Jo didn't even know what a spoon was. We were depressed for days, until we  discovered that all Grace had managed to do was inadvertently flick some gunge at her face with the wrong end of a plastic fork.

So much of the early months of child-rearing took place behind closed doors that it was almost impossible to get an objective idea of how our child was doing compared to everyone else's. Which made the ante-natal class reunion a must. Now, I know I've slagged off these classes earlier on, but at the very least they were a forum for sorting out the able from the less so. And Jo, I'm happy to say, was always one of the most able. Being older than all the other babies may have helped here, but I like to think that I played a part, too. Two days before every reunion I would put her through an intensive revision course of all her skills.

'Remember how to smile? Good. Very good. Practise sitting up now. That's fine. Don't fall over now. I said, don't fall over now.'

'Whaaa.'

'I'm sorry, sweetie, I didn't mean to make you cry. Just don't do that tomorrow evening. OK?'

The first reunion took place when Jo was six weeks old, and at that age she wasn't very responsive to my coaching. Nor was she to my wife's, which was disappointing as breast-feeding was the first competition. Every mother had to sit in a circle and look as though she knew exactly what she was doing. Baby cries, tits out, lock on, and smile beatifically in an imitation of the Madonna and child. I've never been prouder of my wife than I was then. Over the previous few weeks her nipples had been repeatedly savaged by Jo's chomping and were raw to the touch. Did she use her lucky nipple shield? Did she grimace even once? Did she hell.

While the battle of the earth mothers was being fought out in one corner of the room, we dads were left to twiddle our thumbs in another. As ever, when six men are thrown together, the conversation turned to sex.

'Have you started doing it again yet?' said Nick.

What a ridiculous question. Of course I hadn't.

'No. Have you?'

'No.'

'Neither have I,' said Justin.

'Nor me,' said Mark,

'I have,' said Barry.

'WHAT?'

I was shocked. How anyone could even think of having sex before their wife's bits had returned to normal and she could sit down in relative comfort was beyond me. Barry had clearly identified himself as a sexual sadist and I kept my distance from him thereafter.

At subsequent reunions, the contests were more clearly focused on the babies. Who could hold their head up first, who could crawl first, etc. After nine months or so, the thrill of being able to condescend to other parents – 'Don't worry. I'm sure he'll crawl soon. Boys are always a little slower, aren't they?' – started to pall, and I began to get concerned that I had let my enjoyment hinder her progress. While most of the other babies had loads of teeth, Jo had just two. In short, she was severely dentally challenged. Every day I would clamp her mouth open to search for new enamel outcrops, and each day I would be disappointed. I came to the conclusion that her association with slower babies was to blame for her lack of dental development, and forbade her to attend any more class gatherings. History has vindicated this decision, I might add. Jo now has a full set of milk teeth.

FATHER TERESA

By the time Jo was six months old I was fairly clear that there was a right way and a wrong way to bring up children. Alarmingly, most of the other parents were doing it wrong. Everywhere I looked there were children being brought up differently to Jo.

This posed a problem. How much should I allow other people the freedom to make their own mistakes, and how much ought I to be thinking of the child's best interests? For the first time in my life I felt truly in sympathy with a social worker.

Laissez-faire won the day. Intervening was just too much hassle and would be a good way of making sure that everyone hated me even more than they did already, and I salved my conscience by merely giving other parents disapproving looks. You see, apart from anything else it was quite good fun watching other people damaging their children.

In the early days, the trusty old ante-natal class reunion was a fertile ground for this. My wife and I would have a little side bet before the evening started on who could count the most instances of child neglect and ignorance, and as soon as it was over and we were safely out of earshot, the litany would begin.

'Baby Nick was ever so clingy. I don't think he can get much attention at home.'

'Yeah, I noticed that. Did you see how depressed Barry and Sue were?'

I'd had it in for Barry ever since I had discovered he was a pervert.

'Mmm, I did. I'm sure that's why Louise finds it so difficult to socialize with all the other children.'

'Poor kid. And what about Elsie? She's enormous. I'm sure she's being overfed. Every time she cried Justin tried to shove a bottle in her mouth.'

'Depressing, isn't it?'

But it wasn't at all. It was absolutely tremendous to see other parents mess up big time, because it was crucial evidence that we must be doing something better than them. And I only hoped that they carried on the way they were. With any luck, their children would become so inadequate that they would never ever pose a threat to Jo in the future. Well, the job market's bound to be even tighter in 2015 than it is now, and the less potential opposition the better.

Once Jo was up on her feet and running around, I found that taking her to the park was also a great way to feel better about myself. I had to choose my days carefully, though. Weekdays were  useless. One Thursday lunchtime, shortly after Jo had begun to take an interest in the playground, I thought it would be fun to nip out there for half an hour or so. I was pushing Jo on the swings in a bored sort of way when I noticed there wasn't another man in sight. Everyone was either a mother or a child. I felt a frisson of excitement. A sensitive new man out alone with his child; how could they not all fancy me? I immediately put on my best vulnerable yet moody expression and started rehearsing my lines. 'It was terrible. One minute she was walking along the pavement, and the next a lorry had just mown her down.' (Try to cry. Think sad, luvvy.) 'I'm sorry. It's still too painful to talk about.' (Sniff.) 'Still, me and Jo are coping.' (Sniff.) 'But it's hard as a single parent.'

And nothing happened. Not one of those sex-starved mums locked into their loveless marriages said so much as a word to me. Instead they just stared. And it wasn't because they had been stunned into silence by my fantastic physique, I can promise you. To them a single man out alone with a child meant only one thing – a child-molester. The harder they stared, the more selfconscious and clumsy with Jo I became. Which was exactly the sort of proof the mums were looking for. I hung on in the playground for another five minutes – just to show that I had nothing to hide and couldn't be intimidated – and then looked at my watch and said, 'Christ, is that the time?' and sloped off home.

But Saturday and Sunday mornings were a different story altogether. The playground was a curious melting pot of different classes and cultures at the best of times, and striding into it on weekend mornings from the posh side of the common would be a host of Barbour-wearing, green-wellied dads in hot pursuit of their children. And it was these dads that I enjoyed the most, because they didn't have a clue what they were doing. More to the point, most of them hadn't the faintest idea what their children looked like as they hadn't bothered to see them all week. So once their children were running wild with all the others in the playground, the dads were completely stumped. Occasionally one would let out a frantic bellow of 'Edmund' but this wasn't much help as almost every green-wellied dad had a son called Edmund and twelve tiny heads would spin round simultaneously.

Dads like these were good for the soul, because even though I had a better grip on parenting than anyone else I knew, it was nice to get a little reassurance from time to time. You see, between you and me, there were still one or two small areas that I hadn't completely grasped myself. Like how to make sure that Jo knew which parent was to blame when things went wrong.

My wife was out one evening, and Jo and I settled down to do the things we usually did together, now that she was nearly two. A little bit of creative play, a Thomas the Tank Engine jigsaw, followed by a spot of painting. At least that's what I told my wife we had done. Actually, we had just sat down  and watched *The Jungle Book* on video. Come bedtime I had asked Jo if she fancied a bath, and had been thrilled when she had said no. I then left her in her bedroom while I went to get her a new nappy from the bathroom, and when I got back I found her brandishing an open bottle of paracetamol which she had found next to my wife's bed.

Shit. Why hadn't my wife put the lid on properly? OK. Don't panic. Keep calm.

I peered down her throat. No sign of any white chalk. But what if she'd swallowed them whole?

'It's OK, sweetheart, I just need to know if you've eaten any of these pills.'

'Yeah.'

'Is that a yes, you have had one?'

'Yeah.'

'Are you sure? It's very important you tell me the truth.'

'No.'

'So you haven't had any?'

'Yeah.'

This was getting nowhere. There was only one thing for it. Casualty. I left a note for my wife explaining what had happened, and Jo and I set off for the hospital where we had to spend the next six hours waiting to discover that she hadn't ODed.

'How could you? I go out for one evening and look what happens.'

I'd been expecting something like this from my wife when I got back.

'Well, who left the top off?'

'That's got nothing to do with it. You were in charge, and you should have been with her.'

144

We were about to have a full-blooded row, when Jo started to cry.

'Don't worry, darling, Mummy and I were just cross with each other because we had both made a mistake and we were worried about you.'

At the time I felt frightfully pleased with that little speech. It was unusually mature for me, and it did seem to do the trick of calming down all three of us. In retrospect I'm not sure that it was a terribly good idea, though, because my wife and I hadn't both made a mistake. As far as I was concerned the mistake was hers alone, and all my sharing the rap achieved in the long run was to make Jo think she had two incompetent parents.

Thereafter we struggled to get her to do anything she didn't want to. Especially going to bed.

'OK, Jo, it's bedtime.'

'No.'

'Yes.'

'No.'

It was hard to blame her for her reluctance. How did she know that we weren't going to burn the house down, once her eyes were closed? Even so, it was frustrating.

We tried everything. Talking gently and understandingly, talking kindly but firmly, talking sternly, shouting even. We even tried tricking her, by encouraging her to get ready an hour and a half before she needed to. But Jo had a natural sense of timing and made sure that everything took even longer than normal so that she wound up in bed at the same time as usual. Nothing worked. Sometimes she would be as good as gold, and others she would be a pain in the neck, but there was never any correlation to anything we said or did.

Still, there was something to be said for Jo's bedtime moods. At least they happened when none of our friends was around.

SPOT THE PERVE

Before Jo was born I always rather fancied myself as something of a liberal. At college I occupied the administration building and bought the *Socialist Worker* – not as radical as it may sound now, as every student was doing that sort of thing in the seventies, but at least it showed that my heart was in the right place. After I left I was a committed spoilt-ballot voter – well hard, well left – until the late eighties, when I suddenly felt as though my life was slipping away from me and hastily tried to get on the greed bandwagon by remodelling myself as one of Thatcher's children. This lasted about a year, but I was as bad a Tory as I had been a Marxist, so I settled down to life as a wishy-washy socialist and voted Labour.

And then along came Jo to confuse the picture. One night, some time after she was born, the evening news carried a report about a brutal child-murder. Previously when I'd heard such stories I'd been upset, but I'd always been able to programme myself to react along the politically correct lines of 'It must be very tragic for the family, but what about the killer? He must be a very damaged person. I only hope that when he's caught, he gets the appropriate help in prison.' This time, though, I

147

wanted revenge. What's more, I wanted blood. There was no form of death that was too painful for this child-killer. Public executions – *Ja, danke.*

Now, unless you're a member of the Monday Club, sentiments of this kind are not going to win friends and influence people, so I kept quiet and hoped they would go away. Which they did eventually – until the next child-murder, when they promptly returned with a vengeance. I tried to compensate by becoming ever more socially aware in my public outpourings, but nothing seemed to make a difference. There was no getting away from it. Jo had turned the key on my liberal heart, and unlocked the sadistic fascist within.

My thoughts soon strayed disturbingly close to home. If children were getting killed, how could I prevent Jo from becoming a victim? I could clearly warn her of the perils of accepting sweets from strangers, but how could I make certain that she was safe from any of the men I knew? I mean, I bet most of the people who knew Fred West in Gloucester thought he was an OK kind of a guy until the police started digging up his cellar.

At this point, I immersed myself in forensic psychology in order to give myself a good idea of which of my

friends I ought to be looking out for. An extensive reading of the literature offered up the following offender profile of a child-killer: 'A lonely, awkward man, with an elaborate fantasy life and fascinated by pornography.' This was fine as far as it went, but it just happened to be the perfect description of every man I had ever met.

I came to the conclusion that it was just too difficult to put all my male friends under close observation. The real psychos would be far too skilled at avoiding detection to be snared by an amateur sleuth such as myself, and the innocent might get a little narked by my snooping. Worse still, a psycho might even get worried that I was on to him, and hack me and Jo to death just in case.

The answer was to watch my friends' children. By nature they would be more ingenuous than their parents and it should be much easier to catch them out. If their parents were up to any funny stuff at home, I thought, it would be bound to have an effect on them and it would show in their play. Even so, there were always problems of interpretation. Where was the dividing line that tipped brandishing a plastic sword from being mere high jinks to being an unhealthy fixation on the penis?

In Jo's best interests I kept the boy children under far closer scrutiny than the girls. After all, today's charming little lad could be tomorrow's rapist, and, given that Jo's first boyfriend was likely to be the son of someone I knew, I wanted to vet all the suspects. One young boy marked himself out for especial surveillance. Prior to his fourth birthday George had been one of the sweetest, gentlest boys imaginable. As if by magic, the moment he turned four  he became a thug, wholly absorbed in all forms of weaponry. And if he didn't have a gun to hand, he had an uncanny alchemy for rendering the most innocuous of toys lethal. The alarm bells started ringing one evening when Jo returned home after a day out with George and his family.

'Did you have a nice time?'

'Mmm.'

'What did you do?'

'George killed me a lot.'

'What do you mean?'

'He kept shooting me and said I was dead.'

'Did you mind?'

'A bit.'

'So, did you ask him to stop?'

'Yeah, but he wouldn't.'

'So what did you do?'

'I let him shoot me.'

'Why?'

'I like George.'

This boy was evil. No one-shot hitman approach for George; he clearly relished the thrill of long-drawn-out torture. Even more terrifying was his ability to get his victims to enjoy it.

I wasn't sure what to do about George. Under ordinary circumstances I would have had little hesitation in reporting a public menace like him to the authorities, but Jo's fondness for him made that awkward. I knew that any parental attempts to label another kiddy as a 'bad lot' instantly made them more attractive, and that was the last thing I wanted. So how could I end the friendship without being seen to have interfered?

Answer – I couldn't, short of moving house, and believe you me I gave that serious consideration. I tried making out to Jo that a few of the quieter boys were wild, dangerous types, but she wasn't so easily fooled. So I had to let her make her own friends, and hope that her interest in George died a death, so to speak. In any case, when I came to think about it, none of Jo's other male friends seemed much more promising. They were all either besotted with random acts of violence – though none so much as George, it must be said – or silent, neurotic, introverted types. And we all know what happens to them. They start taking drugs. I should know, I was one of them. Maybe one or two of the little boys might grow up into well-balanced adolescents, but it didn't seem likely. Even if one or two of the lads did get lucky, it was impossible to predict at this stage who they would be, so there was nothing to be gained by trying to get Jo to spend more time with certain children. So that was that. If things continued the way they were going, Jo's first boyfriend would probably be a psychopath or a junkie. It scarcely bore thinking about.

Strangers were also a source of constant worry. I could try to stop Jo actively responding to lurking paedophiles or child-abductors, but if one was to make a determined grab for her there would be little I could do about it unless I mounted an armed guard around her every time she went out. And even I could see that was impractical.

I've always been a bit of a coward where violence is concerned. In fact, the only time I've ever been involved in a fight was when a drunk at the next table in a pub mistook my insulting a friend for me having a go at him, and decided to smack me in the face. But now it seemed sensible to learn how to look after myself, just in case I was ever called upon to come to Jo's defence. So I took up kick-boxing circuit training at the gym on Monday nights. This was the perfect contact sport, because there wasn't any. You could stand around looking tough and do exercises that simulated assaults on imaginary people, without ever running the risk of getting hurt.

When I was out walking with Jo and anyone remotely  suspicious started to come near us, I would move swiftly into my kick-boxing routine – leaping into the air while executing power- ful right uppercuts – to deter anyone from having a go at my daughter. And it has worked beautifully so far. No one has bothered us once, not even to ask the time. Violence has a way of creeping up on you, though. After a couple of trouble-free years out on the mean streets, I started to fantasize about someone making a lunge for Jo, and me seeing them off with a few crisp blows. No blood, no gore, no long-term damage; just victory. I wanted to be able to behave like Arnie and Sly, and for Jo to think I was a hero. Creepy, huh? Since when was anyone impressed by Arnie or Sly? Apart from by their bank balances, that is. Time to stop the kick-boxing, I guess.

As Jo's external environment refused to respond to my authoritarianism, my last resort was to impose strict controls at home. Not in the hope of making her any safer, but to make me feel better. On the few occasions in my twenties when I'd thought about having children, I'd always seen myself as a laid-back dad. 'Don't worry about your homework, son, the whole concept's an abuse of your personal freedom. Sure, roll a joint, man, that's cool.' No chance of any of that sort of crap now. The Crace household needed some rules.

Except I couldn't think of any.

You can take the fascist out of the liberal, but you just can't take the liberal out of the fascist.

HAPPY FAMILIES

'Hi, Mum. Hi, Dad.'

'Where's Jo?'

This first meeting with my parents on the hospital stairs a couple of days after Jo's birth was a sure sign that our relationship had changed. No congratulations, no 'How are you?' just, 'Where's Jo?' My parents were no longer interested in me. Jo wasn't an imagined future any more; she was the present, and I was past it. I had been genetically superseded.

In truth, I had rather suspected that this might be the case, which is why I hadn't phoned them immediately Jo was born. Or the day after, for that matter. I felt bad about this breach of birthing protocol, and when questioned about the delay I would always maintain that it had occurred because I was in a state of shock following Jo's difficult delivery. This had the advantage of being partially true – true enough to get me through the family polygraph – but it wasn't the main reason. I was already feeling put out because so much of my wife's attention was focused on Jo, and I wanted to allow myself at least thirty-six hours to get used to the idea before subjecting myself to the double whammy of being rejected by my parents.

Becoming grandparents meant a lot to my mum and dad. They both came from highly competitive families, and late in life the competition had become grand-children. And my mum was falling behind. Over the previous four years, she had regularly been phoned by her brother and sister to be apprised of the latest addition

to their grandchild tally, and would have to grit her teeth and say, 'How wonderful.' My dad wasn't doing so badly. He was locked on nil–all with his brothers.

By the time my wife got pregnant, I think my parents had given up hope of ever getting off the mark. Neither of my sisters had produced, nor showed any inclination towards doing so, and my parents had assumed that I was too incompetent to become a father. They regarded it as something of a miracle that I had survived as long as I had without killing myself, and had tried to look on the positive side of the family line ending with me. At least there would be no more walking accidents waiting to happen.

When my wife and I invited them to lunch to tell them that we were going to have a baby, they could scarcely believe their luck. Nothing I've ever done, before or since, has given them quite so much pleasure. They would be able to cuddle their very own grandchild, they would be able to hold their heads up with their siblings, and they could die happy. My mum and dad have always had a very strong belief in the natural order of things.

You're born, you have children, you have grandchildren, and then you die. Anything else and you've been cheated. And now they weren't going to be ripped off.

So they were in an understandable hurry to see Jo when I met them in the hospital. They had an appointment with a destiny that had yet to be fulfilled, and who knew what might happen to them in the last hundred yards of their journey to rob them of it? A deranged hospital porter might mow them down with a trolley, or a manacled woman prisoner might take them hostage. You never can tell. Their relief on getting to the ward and finding Jo alive and well would have been touching, had it not verged on the rude.

With only a cursory hello to my wife, they grabbed Jo out of her hands and brought out the camera.

'Me first,' said my mum, as she gave the camera to my dad.

Snap. Snap. Snap. Snap. Snap. Snap.

'My turn,' said my dad.

Snap. Snap. Snap. Snap. Snap. Snap.

'How about some of us both together with Jo?' they said in unison, passing me the camera.

Snap. Snap. Snap. Snap. Snap. Snap.

'That's great. Thanks.'

Five minutes later they rather sheepishly remembered that they had forgotten to take any pictures of my wife and me with Jo. And there was nothing they could do about it as they had used up the entire roll of film. Ah, well. Whatever happened from then on, they would always have the photos on top of the TV to prove that they'd been there, seen it, done it.

As the weeks went by my parents learnt to restrain themselves a little. I could sense that they were dying to interfere and tell us how to bring up Jo – we were clueless, after all – but they restricted themselves to phoning every ten days, except when a legitimate pretext presented itself in between. They even learnt to say, 'Hello, how are you?' before inquiring about Jo.

Every now and then my wife and I would take a deep breath and ask my parents to visit. We didn't want to appear too stingy with the invites so we took to asking them when we knew they couldn't possibly come, but this backfired badly when they cancelled a weekend break in the West Country to see us, and we had to revert to being mean. But once I knew they were coming I prepared with care, by practising opening the door quickly and running down the hall to avoid getting steamrollered in the clamour to see the infanta.

Observing my mum and dad with Jo was a strange experience, because it offered the closest insight I was likely to get into how they had treated me as a baby. For years I had been forced to rely on their propaganda of how they had loved me and what they had done with me, because I couldn't remember a damned thing that had happened to me before I was five. My sisters had encouraged me to step off a twenty-foot ledge – rendering me unconscious for twelve hours – when I was two, and then three years later, when it looked as if I was making too full a recovery, they had left the car door open for me to fall out the moment we went round a corner. So I was curious to find out whether it was the two assassination attempts that had made me a neurotic mess, or whether my mum and dad had had something to do with it as well.

Interestingly, it was my dad whom Jo warmed to first. My mum would dance around in front of Jo in a frantic attempt to get her attention and force her to like her, but at three months old all Jo wanted to do was curl up and be held, and since all my dad wanted was to sit down and hold her, they got along just fine together. This arrangement suited me well enough, too, because I was able to drone on to my wife at length about how deprived I had obviously been as a baby, and how my mum had failed to give me what I wanted.

As Jo grew older, my dad's more sedentary life-style wasn't quite so attractive, and my mum began to come into her own. Any game that Jo wanted to play my mum would be up for, and the pair of them would disappear to all corners of the house and garden for hours on end. From a psychobabble standpoint this was an interesting development as it begged the question whether she was trying to compensate for what she hadn't done with me or whether she had actually been like that all the time, but my more down-to-earth view was that it was just plain irritating. It was humiliating both to see that my seventy-year-old mother had more energy than me and to be ignored by my daughter from the moment my mum entered the house.

Jo adored her granny and my mum thought she had died and gone to heaven. No matter how exhausted she became by Jo's attentions, she would fiercely resist any attempts to suggest she take a breather.

'I'm all right.' A lie – she wasn't. 'Anyway, if her granny can't spoil her, who can?'

This was brilliant thinking by my mum because it sounded so plausible. It was only when I thought about it later that I realized it was complete nonsense. Who said grannies were allowed to spoil anyone? Neither of my grannies ever spoilt me.

One of the more enjoyable aspects of having my mum and dad over was that it enabled me to pass off a few barbed remarks about their parenting skills under the guise of having a civilized conversation. 'We never let her cry for more than five minutes without picking her up' and 'Fathers take a more active role these days' never failed to hit the mark. After a year of this, I even became bold enough to criticize them directly. Jo had conned my mum into carrying on doing something with her after she had said she would stop, and I had to put my foot down.

'If you say no, it has to mean no.'

Talk about the child being father of the man. Or woman, as the case may be.

Strangely, my enthusiasm for upsetting my parents diminished as Jo grew older, and I found hidden depths of compassion for them. I realized that they had been two ordinary people struggling to make sense of the world and to bring up their children as best they could. Just like me and my wife.

PARTY BORES

In July 1993 Jo finally made it to one year old. Hang out the bunting, blow up the balloons, freeze the jellies, and let's party. Not.

I've never really seen the point of birthday parties, as their only purpose is to remind you that you haven't died. Yet. Of course I was phenomenally proud of Jo for having survived for three hundred and sixty-five days under her own steam, but there really wasn't that much to celebrate. OK, the risk of cot death was now just about over, and she had had no adverse reactions to the myriad of vaccination courses we had put her through – diphtheria, tetanus, whooping cough, polio, meningitis, plague, etc. – but there were plenty of new worries on the horizon. Such as falling downstairs, getting run over, and Ebola fever. And even if she bypassed all these and went on to have a full natural lifespan, an eightieth of her life was still over.

Worst of all, if Jo was a year older, then I was too. And when you're in your late thirties, that's seriously bad news. We're talking early middle age here. It was bad enough having my own birthday come round every October to depress me, without having Jo's to contend with as well. Still, at least I wasn't as old as my wife. She's always said that being six months older was neither here nor there, but then reality's never been her long suit. Sad, isn't it?

But party is what you are expected to do for your child and party is what we did. Except that we were stupid enough to double the punishment by having two. The trouble had started a couple of weeks earlier.

'I'd like to give a birthday party for Jo.'

The rare occasions when Frances, our first nanny, deigned to stop and talk to us tended to end up costing a lot of money. And this was clearly going to be no exception.

'Seems like a good idea.'

Well – what else could I say? Say no and I get branded as the miserable old git who was too mean to give his daughter a birthday party.

'I'll be inviting all the children that Jo plays with in the week.'

Sounds like she already had.

'How many will that be?'

'Let me see. Mark, Emily, Katy, Joanna, Martha, Frank, Sophie and Tom. And their nannies of course.'

This was more like it. Jo wasn't old enough to play with anyone. In fact she noticed other children only if they happened to nick a toy she was playing with, or they had a toy which she fancied grabbing herself. Almost certainly she couldn't have cared less whether Mark, Emily, etc., came to her party or not. The point of the party was for Frances to invite all her nanny chums to have a good tea and a natter at our expense.

So on the big day our house got invaded by a whole bunch of strangers, and my wife and I were left feeling like outcasts. Nobody at the party knew who we were, nobody cared who we were, and if they thought about us at all they must have presumed that we were staff who had been brought in for the day. Frances had made it abundantly clear that she was running the show, and that we were only allowed to tag along if we handed around the sandwiches and crisps and cups of tea. And like the worthless creatures we were, we meekly complied.

To be fair, a certain amount of lip service was paid to Jo's birthday. The nannies played pass-the-parcel amongst themselves, and when a duck-shaped cake – Jo was very keen on ducks – was wheeled in by me at the appropriate stage, they thoughtfully interrupted their fascinating boyfriend conversations to render a desultory chorus of 'Happy Birthday' before throwing themselves at the cake. Mind you, I did wonder if it might have been better if they hadn't bothered. Jo looked so bewildered by all these faces staring at her, mouthing their tuneless dirge, that I felt sure she would have nightmares for weeks to come. And we knew whom she would wake up. Come to think of it, that's exactly why the nannies did bother.

We'd had an inkling that Jo's party might turn out like this, which is why we'd taken the precaution of organizing a second party, to which only our friends and their children would be invited. This was marginally better, but only just. The one consolation this time was that at least we knew the people who were ignoring us. Seven one-year-olds grouped together in the same room constitutes a death trap, and the parents were so fixated on keeping their little treasures alive that not a word of intelligent conversation passed anyone's lips. This in itself is not particularly unusual among our friends, but they can usually remember the odd 'please' and 'thank you'. Not this time. All we had to show for the pleasure of two hours of our friends' company was the same array of cake and jelly stains on the carpet that we'd had from the nannies.

The only redeeming feature of both parties was the amount of presents that Jo got. Since the nannies were spending their employers' money they were prepared to give generously, as were our friends, who were presumably feeling racked with guilt at the chaos and anomie they were about to cause. So every child who walked through the door came armed with a gift that they were required – often forcibly – to hand over to Jo. And it felt right somehow. Jo was 'the chosen one' and the sight of all her acolytes honouring her in this way was a sure sign that not everything was wrong with the world.

By and large, though, the presents were about as useful as frankincense and myrrh were to baby Jesus. Every parcel seemed to contain some new piece of plastic esoterica that served no discernible purpose whatsoever, despite a liberal sprinkling of words such as 'creative' and 'learning' on the packaging. Did the manufacturers come up with such pointless toys because people actually wanted them, or did people buy them only because they were all there was on the market? Whatever the case, Jo most certainly didn't want her presents. Maybe she was depressed because her birthday had been turned into an excuse for rampant consumerism, or maybe she considered her toys to be genuinely futile, but Jo would take one sneer at a toy and never look at it again. And it would be left to me to round it up and bung it in the toybox along with all the other toys she never played with.

Jo's anti-materialist stance made choosing her a present almost impossible. How could I be sure that my gift would reflect my status as the most important man in her life, and be treated with due reverence? It would be gutting to find that my prezzie had been rejected after a couple of seconds' perusal, while some donation from a complete nonentity got singled out for special attention.

My wife must have been having the same worries, because when I suggested giving a joint present, she leapt at the idea, and under normal circumstances she would have been trying to use her extra spending power to leave me standing. If we were going to be humiliated, then we were going to be humiliated together.

Which is exactly what must have happened, because I have no clear memory of what we gave. If our present had been a success I feel sure that every detail of the ceremonial handing over would have come flooding back, but as it is my mind is a complete blank. Some things are just too traumatic to deal with.

As the years went by, Jo's birthdays became more bearable – at least on a practical level. Her second birthday was still fairly excruciating, but by her third we'd more or less got it cracked. By now she had dropped her heavily Puritan attitude to presents, and was more than happy to be bought. In fact, she insisted upon it. Having given us three months' warning that what she wanted was a badly made, extortionately pricey Snow White dress, it wasn't hard to give her the most rapturously received present of the day.

The party wasn't so bad either. We abandoned any pretence at order, eliminated any games, and let the assorted rabble of three-year-olds get on with it. They could rampage around the garden or help themselves to scoff as they pleased. And all the while the adults slowly – or quickly in some cases – drank themselves stupid on the lawn.

Who knows? I might even enjoy next year's bash.

PLEASE SIR

'So what are you going to do about a nursery school for Jo, then?'

'I dunno. We haven't really thought about it.'

Which seemed perfectly reasonable to me, seeing that Jo was scarcely two years old.

'Well, I think you'd better start. All the good nursery schools are fully booked years ahead. You'll be lucky to get in anywhere.'

Angie, our bossy nanny, was enjoying this. There was nothing she liked better than to expose my parental incompetence.

'Oh, I'm sure we'll find somewhere.'

I wasn't at all, but I couldn't let Angie know that. In fact, I was distinctly rattled. I felt certain that Angie must have rung round all the local schools to make sure they had no spaces left before she bothered to raise the subject with me. Otherwise there would have been no point in mentioning it.

Ten telephone calls on my return home from picking up Jo confirmed my fears. There were no places left. Jo's education was screwed up before it had even started. I blame private schools, myself. I mean, you'd have thought that if you had the dosh you'd have been able to get in somewhere. Apparently not. Nursery schools are every bit as competitive as secondary schools these days.

Being the good woolly socialists that we were, my wife and I initially intended Jo to go to a state school, and had even gone so far as to move close to two schools with good reputations. Unfortunately, we hadn't moved close enough. To be precise, we were 372 metres too far away from one and 457 from the other. At least that's what the schools told us when they wrote to say that they didn't want Jo. Friends of ours in the same predicament had got round this by producing three children in four years and getting listed as 'special needs' status, but that seemed a little drastic to us. So inevitably Jo was going to be consigned to the crap school three miles away on the other side of the borough that nobody wanted to send their children to.

At this point, my wife and I decided to go private. Morally this wasn't too difficult – first off because St Tony Blair of Islington had decreed that private education was just about all right, even for liberals, and secondly because morals didn't really come into it anyway. It turned out that principles about education were what I had for other people's children, not mine. I wanted the best for Jo. I wanted her to fulfil her potential and to enjoy doing it, and if that meant jettisoning thirty-five years of egalitarian thinking, then tough shit.

Financially it was a little harder. We had enough

money to make private education an option, but not enough to afford it without a struggle. Was it really worth committing ourselves to fifteen years of financial hardship just to make sure that Jo could take drugs with a bunch of well-educated middle-class teenagers? After all, nobody's got anything interesting to say when they're stoned, so it doesn't really matter whether they're bright or not. Still, at least if Jo went privately she wouldn't be able to blame her drug-taking on our failure to give her a decent education. In any case, there was also a chance – a long shot, I admit, given her mother – that Jo might turn out normal. Well, relatively normal.

The other big financial worry was that we wouldn't necessarily be committing ourselves to a single set of fees. If we did decide to go ahead and have another child – still very much in the balance at that stage – we couldn't very well turn round to it and say, 'Sorry, pal, we've spent all our cash on Jo so it's the crap school for you.' Out came the spreadsheets and in went all the relevant data – estimated fees, estimated future earnings, and estimated life expectancy of grandparents based on actuarial tables. It all looked a bit of a toss-up, so that's what we did. The coin came down heads, and we decided to take a punt on private.

Which is how we came to find ourselves completely schoolless.

It was time to get tough. Believe it or not, my wife is an even bigger bully than I am, and she took it upon herself to ring round all the schools again to try to make one of them take Jo. Eventually one of the headmistresses cracked. She confessed that she might have a spare place for a couple of mornings a week, my wife said, 'We'll have it,' and that was that.

Jo didn't seem overly bothered about the idea of school when we explained it to her, and as her first day approached it was me who was getting into a state about it. My baby was about to leave home. Even if it was only for a couple of hours or so.

Come the first day, Jo wasn't quite so poised either. My wife and I hung around inside the school for twenty minutes while Jo found her feet, but when it came to saying goodbye it was hard to know whose bottom lip was quivering the most – Jo's or mine.

I went home and tried to do some work, but I couldn't concentrate, and so I stared aimlessly at my WP – just like every other day, my wife would say – until it was time to collect Jo. She was one of the last to appear, and when she did, she looked as though she had just stepped off a particularly nasty fairground ride. Frightened but excited.

'Are you all right?'

'Yeah.'

'What did you do?'

'Nothing.'

And that set the pattern for all future post-school conversations. Even after she had settled in, and – operating on the toe-in-the-door principle – we had soon wangled her  up to five mornings a week, I never could get a damn thing out of Jo about what she had been up to. Once a week she would come home with a folder containing what purported to be her work – drawings, splodges, etc.

– but she was so vague and uninterested in them that they could just as well have been whipped up in thirty seconds by one of the teachers in a bid both to reassure us of her progress and to justify their fees.

I even resorted to trying to trick Jo into telling me, by claiming that the last thing I ever wanted to know was what she did at school, but she wasn't going to fall for that. The only way we had of telling whether she enjoyed school was the absence of complaint. Within weeks she was rushing off into class without so much as a backward glance, and we had to assume that all was well. We came to the conclusion that Jo liked having a part of her life that was distinctly separate from ours. She didn't interfere with my working life by asking me who I had met or what I was writing, and I was to show her the same respect, thank you very much. Her school was her work, and it was nothing to do with me. I have to say that that attitude does not bode well for the future. 'Who were you speaking to on the phone?' 'No one.' And we would both know she'd been speaking to that cretinous dope-smoking boyfriend of hers.

From time to time Jo would let slip the odd enigmatic remark.

'Daisy wouldn't let me play with her today.'

Who the hell was Daisy? This was the first I'd ever heard of her.

'Is she one of your best friends?'

'No.'

'Did you ask her to let you play with her?'

'Yeah.'

Almost definitely a lie.

'Did you mind that she wouldn't let you?'

'A bit.'

Possibly a lie. She could have minded a lot or she might not have cared at all. There was no way of knowing. I'd wrung all the info I was likely to get out of her, and it was time to deliver the responsible-parent homily.

'Well, sweetheart, sometimes people want to do things with other people. It doesn't mean they don't like you.'

But it could do, couldn't it?

Was Jo the most disliked girl at school? I worried a great deal about this. I still haven't forgiven that fat bastard Agnew for making my life a misery at school, turning everyone against me by telling them how wet I was for being homesick, and I lived in fear that the same thing would happen to Jo. Was Daisy her Agnew? I knew I couldn't interfere because that might only make her more unpopular, but I had Daisy's card marked as a bully from that point on. I determined to find out what she looked like, and as soon as I got the chance I would trip her up – 'Oh I'm so sorry' – as she ran out of school. That would serve her right. No one gets away with mistreating her highness.

The nativity play gave us a better indication of where both she and we stood in the general scheme of things.

'I'm going to be the Main Angel.'

Now, I didn't pay much attention to the 'Main' bit as I'm sure all the other angels were also told they were 'Main Angels', but at least she was an angel. There was no chance of her being Mary or one of the wise men or shepherds, because those parts always go to the progeny of parents who have  donated stacks of books and computer equipment to the school, but she wasn't down with the dregs as a donkey or a christmas tree.

Jo was doing OK.

HOLIDAY FEVER

'What shall we do today?'

The rain was tipping down for the fifth consecutive day. For the first two we'd stayed in and done nothing, but since then a combination of cabin fever and one very grouchy Jo had compelled us to dream up some expeditions to pass the time. Such as the theme park with children's zoo, and the children's farm with adventure playground.

'We could try the donkey sanctuary.'

My wife had got to be joking.

'I'll go mad if I have
to look at one more
cutesy animal.'

'It's probably got a
nice café.'

'No.'

'Well, what do you suggest, then?'

'I dunno. How about going shopping in Exeter?'

'What for?'

'Anything.'

'OK.'

Our first holiday since Jo was born wasn't going at all to plan. Instead of the relaxing, sunny, bonding fortnight in the West Country that we had envisaged, we were bored out of our minds traipsing around dull, soggy, so-called tourist attractions. All three of us could scarcely wait to go home.

Yet before we had left we had been congratulating ourselves on arranging this particular holiday. We had deliberately not bothered going anywhere until Jo was up and walking on the grounds that it would be too much of a hassle to push or carry her everywhere, and we hadn't chosen anywhere too ambitious involving air travel or unknown foods that might cause the princess – and hence us – grief.

So where had we gone wrong? Imagining we were going on holiday, that's where. I don't know about you, but whenever I think 'holidays' a certain set of images comes to mind. I think lying by the pool, book in one hand, drink in the other, clear blue skies, wife by my side, World Service on the radio, and idle contemplation of where to eat that night. Pretty dull, I know, but that's me. I think relaxation. And I made the mistake of thinking that I could carry on doing some of that with Jo around. How dumb can you get?

Our daily routine would be as follows. Woken up by Jo between seven – very bad – and eight – very good. Look out the window: rain – very bad; overcast –

reasonable; sunny – never applied. Get Jo dressed. Drive with Jo to buy the papers. Have breakfast. Sit down, but feel too ashamed to put on TV as it's our holiday and we're supposed to be enjoying ourselves together. Decide on somewhere to go. Pay £10 to get in. Mooch around between downpours looking at such exotic animals as pigs, cows, horses, rabbits, etc. Queue up for half an hour in overcrowded café to get a plate of greasy sausage and chips. Mooch around a bit more. Come home for the highlight of the day – Jo's and our rest. Try to persuade Jo to go for a walk, but usually fail as she hates them. Play with her toys while she watches. Make her tea. Give her a bath. Read her a story and put her to bed. Make some supper because we can't go out as we don't know any babysitters. Watch a bit of telly. Go to bed. Not a pool, not a book, not a restaurant, not even a blue sky in sight. Frankly, it was more fun working.

Which made me feel extremely guilty. Why couldn't I just forget my own holiday expectations and get on with enjoying the family idyll? Because I would be in a minority of one, for a start. Every other family I saw at the children's farm seemed to be having as bad a time as us. The parents would look anxious and depressed as they tried to keep their darlings out of the pigsty, and the darlings had seen umpteen pigs before, and would rather have been at home watching something violent on the TV. Yet day after day we kept going back for more. Partly because we couldn't think of anything else to do, and partly out of a sense of social responsibility. We felt it was our duty to clog up the tourist attractions, so that the child-free could relax and enjoy the really nice places without any unwanted noise or interruptions.

There would have been more point to it all if I had thought that Jo was enjoying herself. But I don't think she was. She was separated from her cot, her toys and her friends, and all in all she thought holidays away were a poor idea. She liked the idea of a fortnight with her parents, but why couldn't she have had it at home? Why, indeed.

Time heals many wounds, and one year later my wife had managed to convince herself that the only thing wrong with our last holiday was the weather. So she booked the three of us into a secluded villa by the beach in Corsica, where there wasn't another child, let alone a theme park, for miles around.

This wasn't such a clever idea either. After lugging four bags – one for Jo, one for my wife, one for me and  one for the teddies – plus a travel cot and a push-chair – round Gatwick Airport, and experiencing the naked hostility of other passengers when they discover they will be in the immediate vicinity of a two-year-old for the next two and a half hours, we arrived in Corsica to find the island enshrouded in cloud. And it remained like that for most of the two weeks we were there.

We would wrap up warm and make occasional forays down to the beach, because we'd come to Corsica to have a beach holiday and that's what we were bloody well going to do, but it was hardly much fun. Every ten minutes or so, my wife would look skyward and say, 'Do you think it's going to be like this all holiday?' to which there was no sensible answer, as I wasn't well versed in Mediterranean weather patterns over the previous ten years. So if I was feeling kind I said no and if I was feeling mean I said yes.

Otherwise, we tried to make do as best we could, which wasn't easy as the French hate children almost as much as the English. They could tolerate Jo eating at the same table as us, but that was just about it. As for children's activities – forget it. There was the odd playground with rusting swings and a liberal scattering of syringes, sheared rivets and gravel, but nothing more. The only thing that Jo consistently found entertaining was the musical pony ride outside the supermarket. So most days I would put Jo in the car and drive the five miles to the Intermarché and spend half an hour or so feeding one-franc coins into the pony's head.

Maybe there are some parents who are so inventive and enterprising that they can effortlessly rise above such setbacks and have a good time regardless, but my wife and I weren't of that ilk and we weren't that sorry when the time came to come home. Neither was Jo. As we pulled into our road she said, 'Goody. Now I can see my friends again.' My thoughts entirely.

And so for our next holiday, I roped in two friends, Claire and Tim, and their daughter, Hattie, to come with us. At the very worst we could all be miserable together. To my surprise we weren't. There was as little for Jo to do in the hills of southern Spain as there had been on other holidays, but it didn't matter because she had someone her own age to do it with. She and Hattie were blissfully happy playing and bickering by the pool, and so were my wife and I and Claire and Tim. There were holidays after children after all.

FANCY ANOTHER?

'I think we should start trying for number two.'

'Well, I think we should leave it a bit longer.'

We'd had this conversation at least seven or eight times over the previous nine months, and things were getting critical. Jo was now two and a half and I could feel my wife's enthusiasm for having another baby dwindling by the minute. When we  had first discussed having a second child neither of us had much of a life to speak of. We went to work, we played with Jo and that was that. The start of a new series of *Cracker* was a major social event. So having another baby wouldn't have made too much difference. But ever since her freebie fortnight in South Africa, my wife had become noticeably more child-evasive. And if her rampant hedonism continued unchecked for much longer, I could see that there would be no second baby. It was time to up the ante.

'Why?'

'I just don't feel ready.'

'But you never feel ready to do anything. Besides, if

we wait much longer you'll be too old.'

Not true, but who cared? My wife had a bit of a thing about being older than almost all the other mothers we knew and it was bound to unsettle her.

'I just want three more months. Is that too much to ask?'

Since you mention it – yes.

'What if you change your mind?'

'I won't, I promise.'

She was lying. Three months later my wife got a major promotion at work.

'There,' she said triumphantly, 'I'll be far too busy to get pregnant now.'

It was enough to make me sick. Not just the perfect excuse but an even bigger salary gap to go with it.

'But you promised.'

'Well, I've changed my mind. It's all right for you, you're not the one whose body gets wrecked for the best part of eighteen months.'

Yes, and thank God for that. But it wasn't a debate I was particularly keen to continue, as there was only one winner. And it wasn't me. Best to ignore it and maintain my assault on what passed for her conscience.

'But you promised.'

I kept up this injured-party routine, throwing in a bit

of *faux* sobbing for good measure, for the best part of a week, and by the end my wife had agreed another deal.

'We'll start in the New Year.'

And this time she kept to her word, and a few anxious months later she was satisfactorily up the duff.

I wasn't sure quite why I was so keen to have another child. I mean, it wasn't as if I was so disappointed with the first one that I wanted a replacement. Quite the reverse, in fact. One of my biggest worries was that any second child would fail to match up to Jo. Yet still I wanted another one. I tried to explain it to myself by saying that it would be good for Jo to learn to share and to have someone to moan to about her parents, but this was pure sophistry. Without a doubt, the day another child arrived would go down in Jo's mind as the worst day of her life. No more special undivided attention, no more guaranteed parental knee-space, no more back seat of the car to herself – just bad news all round.

For a while I had imagined that a second child might act as an insurance policy; if anything happened to one child then you would still have one left, and life would be almost worth living. But then I realized that such fatalism was inherently flawed. It just about held good if a disaster befell Jo, but what if it happened to number two?

No, the only logical explanation for having another baby – call me Queen of Hearts if you like – was that I needed someone else to worry about. Clearly my capacity to worry had expanded so much under Jo's expert tutelage that there was now room to accommodate another person. So I'd negotiated one lot of cot-death anxieties. No worries. Or rather, exactly the opposite. There would now be an opportunity to go through them all again. With two children the neurotic possibilities were almost endless. It wasn't just the disease, famine and trauma that could strike them down independently, there was the damage they could do to each other to consider.

'I expect you're rather hoping for a boy.'

Most people seemed to have a zoo-keeper mentality when it came to having children, and our friends and family were no exception. If you'd got one of one sex then it was apparently obvious that you'd want to get the other and complete the set. Presumably if you had another one of the same sex you were meant to swap it. I rather anticipated this attitude from my male friends, as most of them have a touch of the anorak, but I was surprised to find it was equally held by women who had never shown the slightest inclination to file their old copies of *Bunty* 1969–74 in a leatherette ring-binder. But then I remembered that zoos and vets tend to have a lot of women on their staff.

'I don't really care as long as it's all right.'

This is the standard response you have to give on all occasions, no matter how close you are to the person asking the question, and so naturally I obliged. Any other response and people start suspecting you of eugenics if the baby turns out to be what you hoped for, or assume that you're going to hate it if it isn't.

Actually, given the time and effort it had taken to persuade my wife to get pregnant, it was almost true. Almost, but not quite. Deep down, I was worried about having a boy. That's not to say that I didn't entertain happy fantasies of playing footie with my son on the common, but more that I felt safe with girls. I'd been a daddy to a girl for a few years, and I felt I had a fair idea of what to expect from another one.

I knew, for instance, that it was a complete waste of time trying to get a girl to play footie on the common. Because I'd tried. Early on, we'd given Jo a whole load of supposedly male toys, such as balls, Duplo and a train set, but she'd never bothered even to look at them. Yet take her to a toyshop and she had an unerring instinct for the pinkest tackiest piece of Barbie equipment on offer. Put her in a room full of boys playing Power Rangers and she'd be baffled that they wouldn't play Cinderella with her. And all of Jo's little girl friends were exactly the same.

Put simply, I felt that having a boy would be a great deal more difficult. Could I cope with the extra closeness of the mother–son relationship? Could I cope knowing that – according to Freud – my son would be in permanent fear of castration from me? What if I actually wanted to castrate him? Should I put him through the pain of circumcision just so that he had a willy like mine? How would he feel about having a different shaped willy? And that would be only the first few months taken care of.

What scared me most about having a boy, though, was that he might turn out to be just like me, because I didn't feel that I would have the nerves or the endurance of my parents to watch him grow up.

So naturally we had a boy.

ENOUGH SAID

'I've decided that I'm a big girl now and I'm not going to wear a nappy at night any more.'

What a brilliant sense of timing. Jo had previously rejected all our efforts to get her to do this, but now that we were on the way home from the hospital with Tom, her two-day-old brother, she had apparently changed her mind. There was no way she was going to let Tom get all the attention if she could help it.

'That's great.'

There was a little too much enthusiasm in my wife's reply for my liking. There were going to be compensations for her getting woken up by the new baby after all. Such as me having to deal with a wet mass of pyjamas and bedclothes and get Jo back to sleep at any time of the night. But there was nothing I could do except say 'Fantastic' and get on with it.

'Fantastic.'

Within forty-eight hours of three becoming four my life was showing every sign of disintegrating into chaos once more.

Up till then things had gone remarkably smoothly, and I had begun to let myself hope that experience might count for something and that it would be calmer this time. Tom's birth had certainly been a bit easier than Jo's. The presence of two paediatricians on stand-by in the delivery room had been immensely soothing and the midwife had only had to ask a couple of times whether I was OK. It had taken some bullying on my part to persuade the paediatricians to hang around, as the labour seemed to be fairly straightforward, but sometimes neurosis knows best. Sure enough, at the critical moment Tom decided that he couldn't bear the thought of his sister having a more dramatic entry into the world, and proceeded to get into difficulties. The doctors woke up, yanked him out and whisked him off not kicking and screaming to the Neo-natal Intensive Care Unit.

Sometimes déjà vu can be a great help, because it wasn't nearly as frightening the second time round. For one thing, he wasn't as ill as Jo had been – something he will no doubt regret in later life when his sister lets him know how much more he could have milked it; for another, I felt as though the Intensive Care Unit was home from home. With its incubators and monitors and heat, it wasn't the alien environment it had been for Jo's birth but the place where I almost expected my children to be immediately after delivery. In many ways it would have been more of a shock to have found ourselves turfed straight out on to the ward after a trouble-free birth.

Once Tom was alert to the absence of panic he decided to come quietly. He started breathing properly, his blood gases returned to normal, his arm started moving, and within five hours he was kicked upstairs to the hubbub of the maternity ward. Whereupon he went berserk. After the club-class cosseting and pampering of the ICU, he found a more mundane existence extremely trying and he screamed his loudest for hours on end. Eventually the nursing staff suspected there might still be something wrong with him and he was carted back to the ICU. This must have been exactly what he wanted because he shut up immediately – a poor move on his part because he got whisked back to the ward in next to no time. Thereafter he concluded that his best option lay in keeping a low profile, and after a couple of days he and his mum were deemed sufficiently well behaved to be allowed out.

On our return home, we soon settled into a similar routine – or lack of it – to before. Baby cried, panic, then give him some food. If that didn't work, panic, then try to wind him. If that didn't work, panic, then walk him around. If none of those worked, just panic.

There were some significant differences, though.

First off, the phone seldom rang. When Jo was born we had people phoning us up from all over the place to congratulate us, and no day was complete without several visits from Interflora. This time the line went dead. I'd done the good husband bit and rung a long list of family and friends on the day Tom was born, only to be greeted with stifled yawns and, 'That's great, but I must go as I've got someone else on the line.' And that was that. From time to time over the next fortnight a few people, if they hadn't got anything better to do, dropped in to pay their respects to the prince, bringing with them a few half-dead flowers from the petrol station at the top of the road, but it wasn't anything like the flood of devotees that I had been expecting. The message was clear. Having a first child was terribly clever and interesting, but having a second was just plain boring.

'If you move into the spare room for the time being, you won't get woken up the whole time so you won't be too tired to work, and I won't feel bad about putting the light on.'

It wasn't like my wife to be so giving. There had to be a catch.

'Are you sure?'

'Yeah. It makes sense.'

'You don't want me to do anything else in return?'

'Just take care of Jo's night-time wee-wees like you promised.'

No problem.

'And that's it?'

'Yeah.'

'Well, fine. Thanks very much.'

There was, of course, a catch, only I was too literal and stupid to see it. I was surreptitiously getting squeezed out of the relationship. There was a new man in the house and my wife had fallen for his charms. The King is Dead, Long Live the King. It was all horribly Oedipal. The moment the son appeared I was relocated to another room, and he got Mummy all to himself. At least he was only in a cot beside the bed, and not in the bed itself.

Four days later, things took a turn for the worse.

'I think I'll move him in beside me as it'll be a lot easier getting him back to sleep.'

I didn't sleep at all well after that, I can tell you. I was half expecting Tom to wander in and knife me in the back.

It took me the best part of six weeks to wheedle my way back into the marital bed, but even then things weren't on an even keel, as there was Jo to contend with.

At the beginning she had been all sweetness and light, professing how thrilled she was with her new baby brother. But once she realized that Tom wasn't just for Christmas but for life she began to have second thoughts. To be fair she was still quite pleased, but there was a definite edge to her ministrations. When he was asleep there was nothing she liked better than waking him up, and when he wasn't she would wander up to give him the eyeball and then start rocking his chair ferociously. It wasn't that she really wanted to hurt him, it was just that she wanted to let him know exactly who was boss right from the start of their relationship.

The people she really wanted to hurt were me and my wife. It wasn't Tom's fault that he had been born, it was ours. And we had to be punished for it.

And we were. Severely.

Her preferred method of torture was silence. Whenever we asked a question she would act as if she hadn't heard and carry on with what she was doing.

'What do you want for breakfast?'

Silence.

'Hello-o.'

Silence.

'Jo, will you listen to me? What do you want for breakfast?'

Nothing.

Repeat several times. Until—

'Jo, if you don't answer I won't make you any breakfast.'

At which point she would throw a wobbly and dissolve into bucketloads of tears – still not giving an answer.

It was as infuriating as it was heart-breaking. Everything took ten times longer than usual, and any attempts to tell her how much we still loved her and to get her to talk about how she felt about Tom were met with – you've guessed it – silence.

It would all have been a little easier to bear if the punishment had been distributed evenly, but it was me who was getting the brunt of it. Jo clearly considered my wife to be an unsafe target because she was so taken up with attending to Tom that she might just retaliate by paying Jo less attention, while I, who had demonstrated my willingness to be knocked down over and over again and still come running back for more, was fair game. So I got it in the neck.

If I hadn't been so tired, I might have found this flattering, but as it was I just felt sad. Or, to be more accurate, self-piteous. My son had been sleeping with my wife, my daughter was treating me like dirt – just how long would it be before the cat started ordering me around?

And that's when it all started to get a little better. Because to my surprise I found that I actually quite liked my life. Despite the many attractions of a child-free existence – sleep, going out, sleep, more money, sleep, reading the papers, sleep, more money, sleep – I wouldn't change a thing. Well, not much. I even rather enjoyed being woken up at three in the morning by Jo to be told she had wet the bed, because after changing the sheets I could go back to sleep knowing that I had done at least one thing that day that really mattered.

What's more, when I thought about it I didn't mind being number four in the family pecking order. For one thing I realized that I couldn't get any lower. No one, except me, had any time for the cat anyway, so she didn't really count, and there weren't going to be any more babies plummeting me down to fifth. My wife and I were absolutely certain of that. For another, fourth wasn't such a bad place to be, when it was my beautiful wife and gorgeous daughter and handsome son above me.

There. I bet you never expected a schmaltzy ending like that.